ANATOMY
OF A
LAWSUIT

ANATOMY
OF A
LAWSUIT

**What Every Education Leader
Should Know About Legal Actions**

ROBERT J. SHOOP • DENNIS R. DUNKLEE

CORWIN PRESS
A SAGE Publications Company
Thousand Oaks, California

For information:

Corwin Press
A Sage Publications Company
2455 Teller Road
Thousand Oaks, California 91320
www.corwinpress.com

Sage Publications Ltd.
1 Oliver's Yard
55 City Road
London EC1Y 1SP
United Kingdom

Sage Publications India Pvt. Ltd.
B-42, Panchsheel Enclave
Post Box 4109
New Delhi 110 017 India

Printed in the United States of America

Library of Congress Cataloging-in-Publication Data

Shoop, Robert J.
Anatomy of a lawsuit: What every education leader should know about legal actions/Robert J. Shoop, Dennis R. Dunklee.
    p.cm
Includes bibliographical references and index.
ISBN 1–4129–1545–7 (cloth; alk. paper) — ISBN 1–4129–1546–5 (pbk.; alk. paper)
    1. Educational law and legislation—United States. 2. Trial practice—United States. 3. Educators—United States—Handbooks, manuals, etc.
I. Dunklee, Dennis R. II. Title.
KF4119.8.E3S54 2006
344.73'075—dc22   2005015862

This book is printed on acid-free paper.

05   06   07   08   09   10   9   8   7   6   5   4   3   2   1

Acquisitions Editor:	Elizabeth Brenkus
Editorial Assistant:	Candice L. Ling
Production Editor:	Beth A. Bernstein
Copy Editor:	Clara Burke
Typesetter:	C&M Digitals (P) Ltd.
Indexer:	Rick Hurd
Cover Designer:	Michael Dubowe
Graphic Designer:	Scott Van Atta

Contents

Preface

Advisement

This book and the statements of the authors are intended to respond to the professional needs of the reader. The case law interpretation and the presentation of scenarios should not be considered statements of final authority. Only a court of law, guided by individual case facts, can be considered the authority on a specific issue. That issue may be treated differently from court to court and state to state. Legal requirements and accepted customs can and do vary greatly between and even within states and can change often.

This book serves a generic purpose for the education profession and provides only suggested guidelines. While this book is designed to provide accurate and authoritative information in regard to the subject matter covered, it should not be considered a forecaster of impending or future litigation. It should also be noted that any guidelines suggested must be treated with caution in light of the specific subject matter examined and the expected level of personal involvement.

In publishing this book, neither the authors nor the publisher is engaged in rendering legal service. If legal advice or assistance is required, the services of a competent attorney should be sought. In "Annie's Case," all events should be considered fictitious and hypothetical, and any resemblance to real people or specific incidents is coincidental.

Acknowledgments

The authors wish to acknowledge the hard work of, and thank, the SGD Writing Center, especially Sandy, for the exemplary manuscript editing, proofing, and support for us as we developed this book. As always, when we were "muddy" with our words, sentence structure, or direction, they provided the "soap and water" and, when necessary, even bandages for our occasional "authors' egos."

Corwin Press gratefully acknowledges the contributions of the following reviewers:

Frank Brown,
Distinguished Professor
School of Education
University of North Carolina at Chapel Hill
Chapel Hill, NC

Kermit Buckner
Professor, Chair
Department of Educational Leadership
College of Education
East Carolina University
Greenville, NC

Robert A. Frick
Superintendent
Lampeter-Strasburg School District
Lampeter, PA

Jim Hoogheem
Principal
Fernbrook Elementary School
Maple Grove, MN

Gary P. McCartney
Superintendent of Schools
South Brunswick Township Public Schools
Monmouth Junction, NJ

Charles J. Russo
Professor
Department of Educational Leadership
School of Education and Allied Professions
University of Dayton
Dayton, OH

About the Authors

 **Robert J. Shoop, PhD,** is a professor of Education Law, senior scholar in the Leadership Studies program at Kansas State University, and the recipient of the Outstanding Graduate Professor and the Outstanding Undergraduate Professor Awards. He has served as a teacher, community education director, school administrator, and as Ohio State Evaluator of Students Rights and Responsibilities. He is the author or coauthor of fifteen books, including *Sexual Exploitation of Students: How to Spot It and Stop It* (2003), *Sexual Harassment on Campus: A Guide for Administrators, Faculty and Students* (1996) (coedited with Dr. Bernice Sandler), *How to Stop Sexual Harassment in Our Schools* (1994), *A Primer for School Risk Management* (1993), and *School Law for the Principal* (1992).

Dr. Shoop is the coproducer of six educational video programs, including *Sexual Harassment: What Is It and Why Should We Care?*, *Sexual Harassment: It's Hurting People*, and *Preventing Sexual Harassment*. These productions have received national and international recognition, including First Place Award, 1996 National Council of Family Relations Annual Media Competition, 1996 Gold Award of Merit, Houston Film Festival, and 1995 Golden Camera Award, International Film and Video Festival.

Dr. Shoop is a past member of the Board of Directors of the Educational Law Association and has consulted with national associations, community colleges, universities, governmental agencies, businesses, and educational organizations throughout the United States. He is a frequent guest on national radio and television talk shows, including *The Today Show* with both Katie Couric and Matt Lauer, ABC's *20/20*, MSNBC with Lester Holt, CNN, *Day and Date*, *The Jim Bohannon Show*, *The Oliver North Show*, *The Mark Furman Show*, *The Mark Walberg Show*, and *Outside the Lines* with Bob Ley. He is sought after as a speaker at national conferences and has served as an expert witness in over forty court cases. He earned a PhD degree from the University of Michigan

This is the fifth law-related book written by the team of Shoop and Dunklee. Their other books are *School Law for the Principal* (1992), *A Primer for School Risk Management* (1993), *The Legal Manual for Programming Professionals* (1994), and *The Principal's Quick-Reference Guide to School Law,* 2nd ed. (in press).

Dennis R. Dunklee, PhD, is Associate Professor in the Education Leadership Department in the Graduate School of Education at George Mason University. During his 25 years in public schools, he served as a teacher, elementary school principal, junior high and middle school principal, high school principal, and central office administrator. He teaches courses in education law, school administration, and school business management and serves as an advisor and chair for master's and doctoral candidates in school leadership and community college leadership. Because of his expertise and practical experience, he is frequently called on to consult in the areas of effective schools, school law, administrator evaluation, instructional supervision, school-community relations, problem solving, and conflict resolution. In addition, he has been involved as a consultant and expert witness in numerous school-related lawsuits nationwide. As a university scholar and researcher, he has published seven textbooks, two monographs, and more than seventy-five articles on issues in the fields of school law, business management, administrative practice, and leadership theory. He is active in a number of professional organizations, has presented papers at national, regional, state, and local conferences, and is a widely sought-after clinician for in-service workshops.

This is Dr. Dunklee's fifth book for Corwin Press. His other Corwin books are *You Sound Taller on the Telephone: A Practitioner's View of the Principalship* (1999), *If You Want to Lead Not Just Manage* (2000), *The Principal's Quick Reference Guide to School Law* (2002) and *Strategic Listening for School Leaders* (2005) (with Jeannine Tate). He received his PhD in School Administration and Foundations from Kansas State University. His major area of research was in the field of education law, and his dissertation was on tort liability for negligence. He holds a master's degree in Elementary and Secondary School Administration from Washburn University.

Introduction

*After now some dozen years of experience [as a judge] I must say
that as a litigant I should dread a lawsuit beyond almost anything
else short of sickness and death.*

—Learned Hand[1]

Our society has always been drawn to the subject of jury trials
with a mixture of fascination and fear. Because of court-
related stories in both print and visual media, we often tend to associate the jury process with criminal trials. As a school leader in the
world of public, private, or parochial education, you are much more
likely to get involved in a civil trial; however, you are not immune
from involvement in criminal actions. In our profession, the most
common civil cases involve liability for alleged constitutional or
non-constitutional negligence. A few examples of the hundreds of
situations in which school leaders have recently been involved as
defendants, plaintiffs, witnesses, or respondents include:

Criminal defendant—sexual assault

Civil defendant—employment discrimination

Criminal plaintiff—coach assaulted by parent

Civil plaintiff—teacher alleging defamation

Character witness—student seeks diversion agreement

Factual witness—administrator passing in hallway when science
lab explodes

Respondent to interrogatories—principal required to compile and
produce employment records, curriculum guides, test scores etc.

Consulting expert witness—school leaders helping attorneys understand high-stake testing procedures

Testifying expert witness—explaining proper methods of instruction in the use of industrial arts shop equipment

And, as always, hundreds of us find ourselves defendants in negligence suits involving duty, standards of care, improper supervision, maintenance, etc.

"But," you might say, "I took a course in school law. Isn't that enough? Why do I need this book?" Certainly, a basic course in school law required for certification/licensure is important, but such courses typically fall far short of providing us with the knowledge, understanding, and confidence to successfully face a lawsuit. Instead, our law courses are primarily concerned with avoiding lawsuits. This approach to avoiding possible litigation may actually adversely affect our programmatic, personnel, and other leadership decision-making processes and actions, as well as our ability to provide the best teaching-learning environment for teachers and students.

This book will assist you in understanding how:

Litigation works and the jury system operates, and what you can do to assist in the process—that is the process of providing the jury with just the facts—to ensure that the merits of what you did right are noted by a jury, regardless of the plaintiffs' attorneys efforts to make you look like a hapless incompetent

Attorneys work to serve both sides of a dispute by protecting the legal rights of their respective clients. Your job is to support the central focus of this effort by providing honest and forthright information and testimony

You can assist the legal process by being a competent resource in the role of an expert witness

This book describes a classic confrontation between right and wrong. More important, however, whether you are a defendant, plaintiff, or witness, this book can provide you with the tools you need to appreciate and understand:

The special practices of litigation

Its distinctive terminology

The myriad personalities and roles involved

The sometimes intimidating physical environment

Other situations you may encounter in the unfamiliar processes of litigation.

In short, this book will help you view litigation as routine, rather than something that adversely affects your administrative effectiveness in the day-to-day operations of a successful school, and equip you with the confidence you need to focus on students' learning and teachers' teaching, rather than getting mired in efforts to avoid lawsuits at all costs. After all, a lawsuit is often indisputable evidence that you have done exactly the right thing.

When you finish reading this book, we suggest that you place it in your permanent library of "how to" books—in our litigious society you may, unfortunately, need the expertise provided in the near future.

About Section I: A Review of the Legal Environment and the Function of Law

This section briefly reviews the several sources of law and their relationship to the structure and operation of schools and school districts. This review provides the foundation for understanding the manner in which our legal system monitors the education enterprise. When school districts and schools fail to follow the law, or fail to provide a safe place—a place that not only observes the rights of individuals, but also protects those rights—the courts will intervene. Our nation's court systems provide the structure that determines the exact relationship between the individual and the law in question.

About Section II: The Process of Litigation

In this section, you will meet Annie, a third-grade student at Red Ridge Elementary School. Annie was injured in an "accident" during school hours, and her parents filed a suit against the school district that names Annie's principal as one of the defendants. While this hypothetical case centers on eight-year-old Annie, the authors could just as well have chosen a middle school or high school student, or even a teacher, staff member, parent, or school visitor to play the role of plaintiff. This case centers on alleged negligence on the part of Annie's school and school district, but could very well have addressed hundreds of other constitutional and non-constitutional liability issues that educators can and do find themselves answering to in a court of law. The purpose of Annie's case is simply to take you through a typical litigation process.

This section then describes the litigation process, discusses key issues in working with an attorney, and explains the unique atmosphere of the courtroom itself. The purpose is to provide you with insights into the world of litigation that can prepare you to face a lawsuit armed with the background knowledge you need to contribute effectively to your own defense.

Finally, this chapter discusses the inevitable stress that participation in a lawsuit entails and provides some sound advice on how to manage that stress.

About Section III: Verdict and Analysis

This section presents the verdict in Annie's case and an examination of the implications for Annie's school principal and the district.

About Section IV: Serving as an Expert Witness

This section discusses the important role expert witnesses can play in the course of a lawsuit by offering relevant opinions that move the case closer to resolution. The primary purpose of an education expert is to help the court understand the proper operation of schools. This chapter provides information and insights that can help you decide whether or not you might be willing to serve as an expert witness.

About Section V: Managing Your Risk of Litigation

This section briefly discusses how you can reduce your potential risk of litigation by understanding and practicing preventive law.

Note

1. Learned Hand. (1921, November). Address to the Association of the Bar of the City of New York. In *Lectures delivered before the Association of the Bar of the City of New York: Vol. 3. Lectures on legal topics, 1921-1922* (p. 87). New York: MacMillan.

PART I

A Review of the Legal Environment and the Function of Law

1

Why Me?

The vast majority of educators are competent, capable, caring people. Yet even honorable professionals run the risk of making a bad decision or unintentionally causing harm. When someone is injured on school property or at a school-sponsored event, it's important to understand that an educator's intent is irrelevant; it is the impact of the educator's action or inaction that is important. As a school leader, you have to think like a risk manager and objectively assess the potential consequences of every situation. In our litigious society, when people believe that they have been harmed, they look for someone to hold responsible. When the injury occurs in your school or district, this search may well focus on you. The problem facing school districts and, ultimately, you is not whether you are immune from lawsuits, but whether you can develop solutions to minimize your legal liability. Before we turn our attention to the anatomy of a lawsuit, let's take a moment to remind ourselves why lawsuits, and the subsequent litigation, occur in our profession.

Standards of Care

Whether you're a member of a school district's academic team (teacher, director, principal, or superintendent) or a member of the district's support team (secretary, custodian, lunchroom worker, etc.), the

Authors' Note: Some material in this chapter is drawn from "Identifying a Standard of Care," by Robert J. Shoop, 2002, *Principal Leadership*, 2, and is used with permission of the National Association of Secondary School Principals.

prospect of being involved in litigation sometime in your career is clearly possible in today's society. Regardless of the specific incident on which a lawsuit is based, generally, the critical question for the court to decide is whether or not your actions as a school district employee met the standard of care expected for the education profession. If you can prove that your actions met or exceeded the accepted standard of care, you will likely not be found liable. However, if your actions or, in some cases, the actions of your subordinates, did not meet the standards of the profession, you may well be found liable.

In most cases involving an allegation that a school employee has harmed a student (or parent, fellow employee, or patron), the employee's immediate supervisor, i.e. the school principal, is also named as a defendant. In addition, under the concept of *Respondeat Superior*, the superintendent and each member of the district's Board of Education are usually named in the lawsuit[1]. Generally, the plaintiff attempts to show that the alleged harm would not have occurred if the supervisor(s) or other school employees had performed their duties according to the standard of care required of the profession.

In education, as in other professions, the standard of care is the degree of skill and knowledge that can reasonably be expected of a normal prudent practitioner with the same experience and standing. In some professions the professional standards are quite well-established. For example, in medicine, various treatment procedures and protocols are well documented in the literature, and the medical profession generally agrees on the standard of medical care for a given disease or condition. These standards are seldom controversial, and where disagreement does exist, the standards are illustrated by scientific principles; laboratory procedures; and approved, accepted methodologies.

In the field of education, professional standards of care are not only the concern of education professionals and professionals in training, but are issues of real legal liability. The "standard," as understood by a judge and jury, is likely to be influenced by the professional literature and opinions of recognized experts in the field of education administration. Increasingly, the standard of care is being interpreted to mean behavior consistent with recent literature published by recognized authorities in the field of education administration and leadership.

Negligence

Regardless of the specific injury that is alleged, much of the litigation surrounding school administration includes some claim of negligence. Although the law of negligence is a complex area, there are some fundamental principles that apply. People are negligent when they act without due care and attention or they fail to act, and a person whose welfare they ought to have considered is injured by their actions or their failure to act.

Suits for negligence fall under the legal heading of torts—legal wrongs. Negligent torts are historically classified into three categories:

- The direct invasion of someone's legal right (i.e., invasion of privacy)
- The breach of some public duty that causes some damage to an individual (i.e., denial of constitutional rights)
- The violation of some private obligation that causes some damage to an individual

The underlying concept of torts involves the relationship between individuals. Under our system of law, individuals have the right to be free from injury (physical, psychological/emotional, property, financial, etc.) that is intentionally or carelessly caused by others. Negligence may occur in one of three ways: nonfeasance, misfeasance, or malfeasance.

Nonfeasance is the failure to act when there is a duty to act. Nonfeasance is an act of omission, or passive inaction, because of which an injury occurs, due to a lack of the protections that the law expects of a reasonable individual. In order for nonfeasance to result in liability for negligence, a duty to take positive action or to perform a specific act must be established. This duty may be established by a legal statute or by the relationship (for example, principal/teacher/student) between the parties involved. An example of nonfeasance is illustrated by *Gammon v. Edwardsville* (1980). In this case, an eighth-grade girl complained to the school guidance counselor that she feared being physically harmed, based on the verbal threats of another student. The other student was summoned to the counselor's office and was told that fighting would not be tolerated and would result in suspension. Later, in the school yard, the other student struck the complaining girl in the eye with her fist, causing a serious injury. The injured student claimed that the school's response to a given and known threat of violence on school premises was inadequate. The court ruled in favor of the injured girl.

Misfeasance is acting in an improper manner. Misfeasance is taking an improper action when there is a duty to act, and may be either an act of omission or an act of commission. An act of omission is illustrated by *Libby v. West Coast Rock Co. Inc.* (1975). In this case, a student fell into a ditch while attempting to catch a pass in a game of football played during the school's lunch period. The principal was aware of the ditch on the school's property, but had made minimal attempts to warn students and no attempt to fill the ditch. The student was injured and claimed that the school district, knowing of the hazard, did not take proper steps to protect him. The court ruled in favor of the student.

An act of commission is illustrated by *Magabgab v. Orleans Parish School Board* (1970). In this case, a football player passed out on the football field and was treated by school personnel for heat exhaustion instead of the actual illness, heat stroke. The student died as a result of the latter, as well as from the amount of time that the supervisors took before contacting the parents or seeking emergency aid. The court ruled in favor of the parents of the student.

Malfeasance is acting guided by a bad motive. Malfeasance is an illegal act that should not have been performed at all. In the school setting, it can occur when an individual acts beyond the scope of duty. A hypothetical case may illustrate the salient points best. Assume that a teacher administers corporal punishment to a student even though school district policy prohibits corporal punishment. The student is injured as a result of the punishment and brings charges against the school district. The court would likely rule for the student because the act was illegal under school district policy.

The Concept of Foreseeability

Foreseeability is the "degree to which the defendant could have or should have reasonably been able to anticipate the risk of injury or harm to the plaintiff that might result from the action or inaction" (Alexander & Alexander, 2001, p. 560). The expectation of foreseeability regarding the risks inherent in an education setting is greater for educators, because of their superior knowledge, special skills, and professional experience working in an education environment, than it would be for the average citizen who is not professionally trained and experienced as an educator. If you could have, or should have, foreseen or anticipated an accident, your failure to do so may be ruled negligence.

For example, let's suppose that Sally, a sixth-grade student, or even Sally as a twelfth-grade student, slips and falls on spilled spaghetti left on the floor during lunch time in your school's cafeteria. Sally suffers a severe laceration as a result of her fall. The spaghetti, according to other students, had been on the floor for at least

20 minutes. Your duty of care can be understood by answering the following questions:

- Was there a reasonably foreseeable risk of harm for Sally?
- What adult action would have been needed to avoid the harm to Sally?
- Could the adult in question, i.e. lunchroom worker, custodian, supervising teacher, etc., reasonably have been expected to take that action?
- Was the conduct of any person a departure from the standard of care?
- Was there a cause-effect relationship between the negligence and the harm or damage caused?

And what if a teacher (Steve) who went to help Sally also slipped and fell? As a result of his fall and his efforts to help Sally, Steve suffered severe and long-term back injuries that may prevent him from returning to work. The same questions would apply to determine your duty of care regarding Steve. You can use those five basic questions in assessing your own liability in any situation in which a child, adult, or even a visitor is physically injured while under your sphere of supervision.

The concept of foreseeability expects you to perform as a reasonably prudent person of similar training and circumstances should perform. This degree of care is based on the relative age, training, maturity, and experience, as well as any other related characteristics of the educator. The law does not require you to be able to predict everything that might happen in the immediate future, nor do the courts require the educator to completely ensure the safety of students and others. Courts do, however, expect you to act in a reasonable and prudent manner. If the ordinary exercise of prudence and foresight could have prevented an accident that caused an injury, courts have ruled educators negligent.

Your *In Loco Parentis*[2] Duty as a School Leader to Provide a Safe Learning Environment

Our society generally assumes that during the time a student is away from home and involved in school activities, the student's interests, welfare, and safety are directed by, and under the control of, reasonable, responsible, trained adults. As a school leader, you are responsible for the safety and welfare of the students placed in your care, custody, and control.

Education reform literature emphasizes that a safe and orderly learning environment is essential for learning. The professional literature further holds that building administrators (principals and assistant principals) are the most important players in ensuring a positive learning environment. You are responsible for supervising students, teachers, and support staff, and for ensuring that your school is a safe and healthy place to learn. You are also responsible for ensuring compliance with all school district policies and state laws.

Some negligence cases against school districts have been based on the argument that the school has a constitutional or statutory duty to protect students because of a "special" relationship between the child and the school. Although this argument is frequently put forward, courts, in general, have not been willing to extend the protection of the special relationship with schoolchildren infinitely. While laws mandate school attendance, the courts have generally agreed that the state has not assumed responsibility for the children's entire lives. Children and their parents retain substantial freedom to act and are responsible for their actions.

Section 1983

Section 1983 of the Civil Action for Deprivation of Rights Act is one of the most commonly used causes of action to redress violations of federal constitutional rights by government officials. Section 1983 holds "every person" acting under color of state law liable for depriving any other person in the United States of "any rights, privileges, or immunities secured by the Constitution and laws[3]." To recover damages against a government official under section 1983, a plaintiff must establish that:

- A constitutional right existed.
- The defendant violated that right under color of state law.
- The defendant's act is the proximate cause of the plaintiff's injury.

Plaintiffs can bring a successful action under section 1983 if individuals acting under color of state law deprived them of a constitutional right, and they were deprived of their constitutional rights without the due process of law. Although individuals who violate someone's rights while acting outside the scope of their authority may be held personally liable, section 1983 provides qualified or conditional immunity from civil prosecution to individuals as long as they are acting clearly within the scope of their authority.

Knowing and Assimilating Your School District's Policies and Procedures

One of the clearest statements of your duties and standard of care, as a school leader, is contained in your school district's official policies and procedures. In the event that a complaint is filed against you, the first question likely to be asked is whether or not your action (or inaction) was in compliance with district policies and procedures. To the extent that they were, your personal liability will certainly be limited, since you were acting in a prudent manner. It's important, therefore, that you be fully cognizant of your district's policies and procedures and ensure that you and your faculty and staff follow them at all times.

Ethics Versus the Law

The distinction between ethical and legal issues is often vague. Ethical concepts become legal principles only when a legislature enacts a specific law or a court publishes a decision. If there is a conflict between your ethics and the law, you are bound to comply with the law. For example, in a case of suspected child abuse, you may know and understand the state's child abuse law, but be reluctant to report your suspicion because you don't want to risk damaging another person's reputation without "proof of abuse." Every state has a statute that identifies school leaders as mandatory reporters of "suspected" child abuse. Based on your sense of ethics and fairness, you may be tempted to personally investigate the situation before reporting the suspected abuse to state authorities. However, laws override ethical principles, which do not have the strength of law. You must report the suspected abuse, even at the risk of harming an innocent person's reputation.

Sometimes your personal loyalties can conflict with your legal duty. You have an affirmative responsibility, no matter what the consequences may be, to provide a learning/teaching environment that's as safe as possible. If you have knowledge of practices or procedures that are legally questionable, you must make every effort to observe the employee whose behavior is questionable and to advise him or her to immediately cease that behavior. However, once a formal complaint has been discussed or filed, you must refrain from any actions that could be construed as interference with an impending or ongoing investigation by appropriate authorities.

What Constitutes Acceptable Behavior by You as an Education Professional

In the final analysis, what constitutes acceptable behavior for education leaders is decided by society, as represented by federal and state constitutions, federal and state statutes, administrative law, local district policy, court-made law, standards of the profession, and the "best practice of the profession," as presented by various professional organizations and other recognized authorities in the field of education.

The three sources of law that most directly affect the operation of schools are statutes, administrative law, and case, or common, law. Statutes are laws enacted by state or federal legislatures. Administrative laws are regulations promulgated by administrative agencies (the U.S. Department of Education, state boards of education, etc.). Both are published after enactment. Statutes are considered the primary source of law. School leaders are expected to know and obey all of the laws and regulations that control the operation of schools.

In contrast to statutes, common law, or case law, is the body of judge-made law (e.g., legal decisions that interpret prior case law and statutes). Experts believe that statutes are not law until they have been tested and adjudicated in a court of law. When a court is confronted with an issue that can't be resolved by reference to pertinent statutory or administrative law, it decides the case according to common law.

The common law tradition interprets how laws are to be understood. Case law follows the doctrine of *stare decisis* (to stand by things already decided), in which lower courts make decisions that are consistent with the decisions of higher courts, under the principle of "precedent." Common law is not automatic but must be applied by a court. When courts decide specific disputes, they examine constitutional, statutory, and administrative law. The court determines the facts of the case and then examines prior judicial decisions to identify legal precedents.

After federal and state statutes and legal precedents, standards of professional organizations and professional literature are the most common sources for definitions of duty and standards of care. These professional standards are often used to delineate or benchmark the expected standard of care. During the testimony of a school district employee in a court case, it is a common practice for the plaintiff's attorney to ask the employee to agree that a certain source is authoritative. For example, the attorney might say, "Mr. Jones, as principal of Shady Brook High School, do you agree that the National Association of Secondary School Principals is the leading professional organization for secondary school principals?" Once it is established that Principal Jones agrees that the National Association of Secondary School Principals (NASSP) is a nationally respected association for school administrators, the attorney then attempts to point out where Jones' behavior did not conform to the standards presented in various documents from this organization. (Note: Other principals' organizations, such as the National Association of Elementary School Principals, have similar published standards.)

In recent years, several sets of comprehensive standards have been developed to guide the professional development of school leaders. One of the earliest of these standards is *Guidelines for the Preparation of School Administrators*, published by the American Association of School Administrators in 1983. These guidelines were followed by two significant NASSP publications: *Performance-Based Preparation of Principals: A Framework for Improvement* (1985) and *Developing School Leaders: A Call for Collaboration* (1992). In 1990, the National Commission for the Principalship published *Principals for Our Changing Schools: Preparation and Certification* and the National Association of Elementary School Principals published *Principals for the Twenty-First Century*. These publications paved the way for the subsequent standard-building work of the National Policy Board for Educational Administration (NPBEA). NPBEA is a consortium of associations representing the education administration profession.[4]

As a result of two decades of collaborative research, two publications have emerged that include what are generally accepted as the performance standards for principals. These standards are included in *21 Performance Domains of the Principalship* (1992), produced by NPBEA, and *Six Standards for School Leaders* (1996), developed by the Interstate School Leaders Licensure Consortium (ISLLC).

Both of these publications identify benchmarks against which a principal's performance will likely be measured. ISLLC Standards 5 and 6 address the relationship of the standards to practice. Standard 5 states that "a school administrator is an educational leader who promotes the success of all students by acting with integrity, fairness, and in an ethical manner" (Council of Chief State School Officers, 1996, p. 18). This standard has been interpreted to mean that an administrator has knowledge and understanding of the purpose of education, the role of leadership in modern society, and the values of the diverse school community. Consequently, the administrator

> serves as a role model, accepts responsibility for school operations, considers the impact of one's administrative practices on others, treats people fairly, equitably, and with dignity and respect, protects the rights and confidentiality of students and staff, demonstrates appreciation for and sensitivity to the diversity in the school community . . . [and] will demonstrate integrity and exercise ethical behavior, and applies laws and procedures fairly, wisely, and considerately. (Skarla, Erlandson, Reed, & Wilson, 2001, p. 112)

Standard 6 states that "a school administrator is an educational leader who promotes the success of all students by understanding, responding to, and influencing the larger political, social, economic, legal and cultural context" (p. 19). This standard has been interpreted to mean that an education leader

> "Know[s] the law as it relates to education and schooling"
>
> Is "committed to using legal systems to protect student rights and improve student opportunities"
>
> Is required to "work within the framework of policies, laws, and regulations enacted by local, state, and federal authorities"
>
> "Promotes the success of all students by understanding, responding to, and influencing the larger political, social, economic, legal, and cultural context"
>
> Recognizes the importance of diversity and equity in a democratic society
>
> Facilitates process and engages in activities ensuring that the school community works within the framework of policies, laws, and regulations enacted by local, state, and federal authorities. (Skarla et al., 2001, pp. 122–123)

As a school leader, to manage your personal and professional risk of litigation, you should know, at a minimum:

- The state statutes that govern the operation of a school
- School board approved policies and procedures
- Leading state and federal court cases that govern the operation of the school.

References

Alexander, K., & Alexander, M. (2001). *American public school law*. Belmont, CA: West/Wadsworth.

Bethel School District No. 403 v. Fraser, 478 U.S. 675 (1986).

Civil Action for Deprivation of Rights Act , 42 U.S.C. § 1983 (1979).

Council of Chief State School Officers. (1996). *Interstate School Leaders Licensure Consortium standards for school leaders*. Washington, DC: Author.

Garcia v. City of New York, 646 NYS2d 509 (1996).

Gammon v. Edwardsville School District, 82 Ill. App. 3rd 586, 589, 403 NE2d (1980).

Libby v. West Coast Rock Co., Inc. 308 So. 2d 602 (Fla 2d DCA 1975).

Mohabgab v. Orleans Parish School Board, 239 So 1d 456 La Ct App (1970) 36.

Skarla, L., Erlandson, D., Reed, M., & Wilson, A. (2001). *The emerging principalship*. Larchmont, N.Y: Eye on Education.

United States v. Classic, 313 U.S. 299 (1941).

Notes

1. *Respondeat Superior*: Based on English common law, this doctrine holds that a master is liable in certain circumstances for the negligent acts of his servant if the negligent acts occurred in the course of employment. Courts have generally held the employer liable only for actions that are outrageous, motivated by personal interests, or not serving a rational business purpose, or where the employer deliberately remained ignorant of criminal conduct. The contemporary justification for this doctrine is that if an employer knows that it may be held liable for the actions of its employees, it is more likely to exercise care in the selection, employment, and supervision of its employees.

2. *In Loco Parentis*: The doctrine of in loco parentis holds that when children leave the protection of their parents, the school takes over physical custody and control of the children and effectively takes the place of their parents (*Garcia v. City of New York*, 1996). The U.S. Supreme Court acknowledged there is an "obvious concern on the part of parents, and school authorities acting in loco parentis, to protect children . . ." (*Bethel School District No. 403 v. Fraser*, 1986).

3. To act "under color of state law" means to act beyond the bounds of lawful authority, but in such a manner that the unlawful act is done while the official is purporting or pretending to act in the performance of his or her official duties. In other words, the unlawful act must consist of an abuse or misuse of power that the official possesses only because he or she is an official. For example, "Misuse of power, possessed by virtue of state law and made possible only because the wrongdoer is clothed with the authority of state law, is action taken 'under the color of' state law." (*United States v. Classic*, 1941).

4. The NPBEA consortium includes: American Association of Colleges for Teacher Education, Association of School Business Officials, Council of Chief State School Officers, National Association of Secondary School Principals, National School Boards Association, American Association of School Administrators, Association for Supervision and Curriculum Development, National Association of Elementary School Principals, National Council of Professors of Educational Administration, and University Council for Educational Administration.

5. For a detailed discussion of the 21 Performance Domains that define the basis for exemplary principal performance, see Skarla et al. (2001).

2

The Legal Environment and Organization of the Courts

This chapter briefly reviews the legal environment in which lawsuits take place. While we've all had some exposure to this information in high school or college courses, this review provides an important foundation for the chapters that follow.

The Function of Law

The function of law is to regulate human conduct in order to ensure a harmonious society. Legislators and courts are continuously involved in the effort to strike a balance between individual freedom and society's need to function without unreasonable interference from the conduct of individuals. The United States Constitution provides particular protections for individual rights. Various state and federal statutes protect the general welfare of society and implement the constitutional rights of individuals.

Our system of government provides a structure of laws that protects individual rights and guarantees freedom of religion, speech, press, and assembly, and the right of each individual to call upon the courts or government to correct injustices. There are separate legal systems for each of the fifty states, the District of Columbia, and the federal government. For the most part, each of these systems applies its own body of law.

A law is a rule of civil conduct prescribed by local, state, or federal mandates, commanding what is right and prohibiting what is wrong. Laws, then, are simply collections of those rules and principles of conduct that the federal, state, and local communities recognize and enforce. Our system of laws is based on the assumption that all citizens should be held to the same standards of behavior and that there are certain consequences for individuals who fail to meet those standards.

The court systems provide the structure that determines the exact relationship between the individual and the law in question. In our legal system, the principle of due process of law allows people who have been accused of breaking a law or harming another person, and people who have been harmed by other individuals, to bring their side of the issue before a court to decide whether they must submit to the force of government or be protected by it.

Our government is based on the consent of the governed, and the Bill of Rights denies those in power any legal opportunity to coerce that consent. Authority is to be controlled by public opinion, not public opinion by authority. This is the social compact theory of government. Because of this, law is not a static set of printed documents, but a living and changing set of precepts that depend on the courts for interpretation.

Laws are divided into two broad classifications: civil and criminal. Criminal law regulates public conduct and prescribes duties owed to society. Civil law regulates relations between individuals.

Sources of Law

Constitutional Law

In the United States, law is composed of constitutional law, common law, statutory law, and administrative law. Whether at the federal or state level, a constitution is the basic source of law for the jurisdiction. Constitutions specify the structure of the government and identify the powers and duties of its principal officers and subdivisions. They also designate the allocation of power between levels of government—between the federal government and the states (the United States Constitution), and between state and local governmental bodies (state constitutions). In addition, constitutions spell out the exact limitations of governmental power. In both the United States Constitution and state constitutions, these proscriptions are contained in a bill of rights.

Constitutions are broad philosophical statements of general beliefs. The United States Constitution is written in such broad and general language that it has been amended only twenty-six times in more than two hundred years. State constitutions are more detailed and specific, with the result that most are frequently amended. Just as the United States Constitution is the supreme law in the United States, the state constitution is the supreme law within each state. State constitutions may not contain provisions, however, that conflict with the United States Constitution.

Because the United States Constitution contains no mention of education, Congress is not authorized to provide a system of education. The Tenth Amendment to the United States Constitution stipulates that "the powers not delegated to the United States by the Constitution, nor prohibited by it to the states, are reserved to the states respectively, or to the people." The United States Supreme Court has repeatedly and consistently confirmed the authority of states to provide for the general welfare of their residents, including the establishment and control of their public schools. However, the United States Supreme Court has applied various provisions of the United States Constitution to jurisdictions to ensure compliance.

The following Article, commonly referred to as the United States Constitution's General Welfare Clause, and Constitutional amendments contain provisions of special interest to education leaders:

General Welfare Clause: Under Article 1, Section 8 of the Constitution, Congress has the power to "lay and collect taxes, duties, imports and excises, to pay the debts and provide for the common defense and general welfare of the United States." Congress has often used the General Welfare Clause as the rationale for the enactment of legislation that directly impacts the operation of public schools. Examples include the Head Start program, special education laws, and the No Child Left Behind Act (2002).

First Amendment: The First Amendment states that "Congress shall make no law respecting an establishment of religion, or prohibiting the free exercise thereof, or abridging the freedom of speech, or of the press; or the right of the people peaceably to assemble, and to petition the Government for a redress of grievances." This amendment affords pervasive personal freedom to the citizens of this country. It has been used as the basis for litigation involving the use of public funds to aid non-public school students, separation of church and state in curriculum matters, students' and teachers' freedom of speech, press censorship, and academic freedom issues.

Fourth Amendment: The Fourth Amendment protects the rights of citizens "to be secure in their persons, houses, papers and effects against unreasonable search or seizure." This amendment emerged in the late 1960s as the basis for litigation concerning the search of students' lockers and personal belongings.

Fifth Amendment: The Fifth Amendment protects citizens from being compelled, in criminal cases, to be witnesses against themselves. Although most due process litigation concerns the Fourteenth Amendment, several self-incrimination issues have been raised in cases concerning teachers being questioned by superiors regarding their activities outside the classroom.

Sixth Amendment: The Sixth Amendment guarantees a citizen "the right to a speedy and public trial, by an impartial jury . . . to be informed of the nature and cause of the action; to be confronted with the witnesses against him; to have compulsory process for obtaining witnesses in his favor, and to have the assistance of counsel for his defence [*sic*]." In combination with the Fourteenth Amendment, this amendment provides the basis for due process policies and procedures used by school systems.

Fourteenth Amendment: The Fourteenth Amendment provides that no state shall "deny to any person within its jurisdiction the equal protection of the laws" (Section 1). This amendment is frequently cited in education cases that deal with race, gender, or ethnic background issues. Recent cases regarding disabilities and school finance issues also have been based on this amendment. As a corollary, this amendment guarantees the right of citizens to due process under the law, and thus has been used to support school employees' claims of wrongful discharge and parents' claims of unfair treatment of their children by school officials.

Because education is a state function and responsibility, the state legislature has plenary (absolute) power to make laws governing education. The state legislature also has complete authority to modify the laws regulating education. These laws grow by the accumulation of custom, constitutional provisions, existing laws, moral principles, and community standards. However, statutes can't override constitutional authority.

Common Law

When confronted with a problem that can't be solved by reference to pertinent legislation (statutory law), a court decides the case according to common law. Common law is defined as those principles, procedures, and rules of action enforced by courts that are based on history or custom and modified, over time, as required by circumstances and conditions.

Common law is not automatic but must be applied by a court. Courts decide specific disputes by examining constitutional, statutory, or administrative law. When there is a question of the applicability of existing laws and regulations, the court determines the facts of the case and then examines prior judicial decisions to identify legal precedents (if any exist).

Statutory and Administrative Law

Statutes are laws passed by a legislative body. These laws may alter common law by adding to, deleting from, or eliminating the common law precedent. Under our system of government, the courts are the final interpreters of legislative provisions.

Administrative laws are regulations promulgated by administrative agencies. An administrative agency is a governmental authority, other than a court or legislative body, that affects the rights of private parties through adjudication or rule making. In many cases, the operations of schools are affected more by the administrative process than by the judicial process. It is not uncommon for a state to have several hundred agencies with powers of adjudication, rule making, or both.

Structure of Government

It is the American ideal that the power to control the conduct of people by the use of public will is inherent in the people. This is accomplished by the adoption of a constitution through which the people delegate certain powers to the state. Constitutions divide this power and assign it to three separate but equal branches of government.

Although no one branch performs only one function, each branch has a generally defined area of influence. The legislative branch makes the laws. The judicial branch interprets the law. The executive branch enforces the law.

The Legislative Branch

The legislative branch is created constitutionally with the primary function of making laws. It is limited in its function only by the state and federal constitutions. Each state legislature has the absolute power to make laws governing education. It is important to understand that this makes education a state function, makes school funds state funds, and makes school buildings state property.

Although the state legislature can't delegate its lawmaking powers, it can delegate to subordinate agencies the authority to make the rules and regulations necessary to implement these laws. One such subordinate agency is the state board of education.

State boards of education are the policy-making and planning bodies for the public school systems in most states. They have specific responsibility for adopting policies, enacting regulations, and establishing general rules for carrying out the duties placed on them by state legislatures. Local school districts and local boards are created by the state legislature, and have only those powers that are specifically delegated by the legislature or that can be reasonably implied.

The Executive Branch

Although each state has a unique structure, the typical executive branch includes a governor, a lieutenant governor, a secretary of state, a treasurer, and an attorney general. The governor is the chief executive officer of the state and is responsible for the enforcement of the laws of the state. The attorney general is a member of the executive branch of government who often has significant impact on the operation of schools in the state. The attorney general represents the state in all suits and pleas to which the state is a party; gives legal advice, when requested, to the governor and other executive officers; and performs such other duties as may be required by law.

The attorney general acts as both the defender and the prosecutor of the state's interest. The attorney general acts for the state much as a private attorney acts on behalf of a private client and renders opinions on questions of interest to the state submitted by state officials. In such opinions, the attorney general identifies the laws applicable to the question and the set of facts presented. These opinions are not laws or court decisions; they are interpretations of state law that are enforceable in the absence of a contrary court ruling.

The Judicial Branch

Courts interpret laws and settle disputes by applying the appropriate law. However, a court can decide a controversy only when it has authority to hear and adjudicate the case. Prior to any litigation, a lawyer must decide whether to file at the state or federal level, and in which particular court—magistrate, district, or supreme court. The appropriate jurisdiction emanates directly from the law. Court names vary from state to state. For example, trial courts are called supreme courts in New York, circuit courts in Missouri, and district courts in Kansas.

The principal function of the courts is to decide specific cases in light of the Constitution and the laws. In each state, there are two judicial systems that operate simultaneously: the federal court system and the state courts. Courts in both systems are classified as having either original or appellate jurisdiction.

Original jurisdiction refers to the right of a court to hear a case for the first time. A trial on the facts occurs in a court of original jurisdiction. Once the initial trial is over and a judgment rendered, the appellate process may begin.

Appellate jurisdiction refers to the right of a court to hear cases on appeal from courts of original jurisdiction. In appellate courts, matters of fact are no longer in dispute; instead, questions of law or proceedings from the lower courts serve as the basis for review. The appellate process can proceed to the state's highest court or to the United States Supreme Court.

The Federal Court System

The federal court system of the United States includes district courts, special federal courts, courts of appeal, and the Supreme Court.

Federal District Courts

There are 97 federal district courts, with at least one in each state, the District of Columbia, the Virgin Islands, and Puerto Rico. Each district court has a chief judge and other federal judges appointed by the President. These courts have original jurisdiction in cases between citizens of different states where an amount of money over $10,000 is in dispute, and in cases involving litigation under federal statutes or the United States Constitution. The district courts have no appellate function. Appeals from the district courts are made to the courts of appeal in the respective circuits.

In some limited circumstances, a special three-judge district court can be convened to decide a controversy. This type of tribunal is used when a state statute is being challenged under the United States Constitution. A special application must be made to the district court; if granted, the chief judge and at least one other judge must be from the court of appeals. The importance of this type of tribunal lies in the fact that an appeal of its decision goes directly to the United States Supreme Court.

There is a chief judge designated for each federal district court and other judges as authorized by federal law. The judges hold their office for life "during good behavior."

Federal Courts of Appeal

The first level of appeal in the federal court system is in the courts of appeal. These courts provide an intermediate level of appeal between district courts and the Supreme Court. These courts have only appellate jurisdiction and review the record of the trial court for violations of legal proceedings or questions of law, rather than questions of fact. The courts of appeal operate with several judges. There is no jury; a panel of three or more judges decides the cases before them. In some cases, the judges may sit *en banc* (together) to decide the case. There are 12 federal circuits in the United States, each with a court of appeals.

United States Supreme Court

The United States Supreme Court alone among the federal courts was created directly by the Constitution, rather than by federal legislation. This court consists of the Chief Justice and eight Associate Justices. It has limited original jurisdiction, and exercises appellate jurisdiction over federal district courts, federal courts of appeal, and the state supreme courts.

The Supreme Court is the nation's highest court. It is often referred to as "the court of last resort" in that there are no appeals to its decisions. Of course, a constitutional amendment ultimately could be used to reverse this court's decision; however, this has occurred in only four instances. Since more than 5,000 cases are appealed to the Supreme Court each year, the Court most frequently will deny *certiorari* and refuse to review the decisions of the lower courts. The denial of *certiorari* has the effect of sustaining the decisions of the lower courts.

The State Court System

The system of state courts varies from state to state and no two states have identical systems. In general, however, the states, like the federal government, have a hierarchically organized system of general courts along with a group of special courts.

The lowest level of state courts, often known generically as inferior courts, may include any of the following:

magistrate court

municipal court

justice of the peace court

police court

traffic court

county court

Such courts usually handle minor civil and criminal cases. More serious offenses are heard in superior courts, also known as state district courts, circuit courts, or by a variety of other names. The superior courts, usually organized by county, hear appeals from the inferior courts and have original jurisdiction over major civil suits and serious crimes. It is here that most of the nation's jury trials occur. The highest state court, usually called the appellate court, state court of appeals, or state supreme court, generally hears appeals from the state superior courts and, in some instances, has original jurisdiction over particularly important cases. A number of the larger states, such as New York, also have intermediate appellate courts between the superior courts and the state's highest court.

States may also have any of a wide variety of special courts that may include:

juvenile court

divorce court

probate court

family court

housing court

small claims court

In all, there are more than 1,000 state courts of various types that handle the overwhelming majority of trials held in the United States each year.

Function of the Courts

The primary purpose of courts is to ensure that every person has a fair and unbiased trial before an impartial arbiter. The courts have the power to decide an issue, including the power to decide it wrongly. If a wrong or erroneous decision is made, it is the option of the losing party to acquiesce to or appeal the decision. The purpose of an appeal is not to dispute the right of the court to make a decision, but to review the trial evidence and the applicable laws to determine whether or not the litigant has been given a fair trial.

It is assumed that there are always conflicting interests and that the courts must weigh one against the other. Often, the decision is not between good and bad, but is a matter of selecting the greater good or the lesser evil.

Courts have three general functions: deciding controversies, interpreting enacted law, and judicial review. Deciding controversies consists of determining the facts of the dispute and applying the applicable law. There may be one or more statutes or regulations that apply. If there are none, the court must decide the controversy based on previous decisions of the appellate courts of the state in similar situations. If the case presents a new situation, the court's job is more difficult. When a court does not wait for legislative action and makes a decision, it has, in fact, made a new law. In this process, *stare decisis*, or the adherence to precedent, creates a new foundational common law.

Interpretation of enacted law occurs when a statute doesn't provide a clear answer to the question before the court. Because it is not always possible to draft legislation that is unambiguous when applied to specific controversies, a court may be forced to strike down a statute that it feels is vague, ambiguous, or contradictory. The courts tend to use the following approaches in interpreting legislation:

Literal: The courts look to the ordinary interpretation of words to determine their meaning.

Purposive: The courts attempt to ascertain what the legislature intended the law to mean.

Precedent-based: The courts look to past similar cases and laws to find support for one interpretation of the law.

Policy-based: The courts interpret the law in relationship to the courts' own view of what is best for society.
The courts often adopt a combination of these approaches in making their decision.

Judicial Review is a supreme court's power to declare that a statute is unconstitutional. This power has led some to say that the judicial branch is the first among the three equal branches of government. However, this power is not without its limits. Judges at all levels are expected to base their decisions on precedents under the legal doctrine of *stare decisis.* This means that the court must look to other decisions in similar cases in dealing with new cases.

Alternative Dispute Resolution

Alternative dispute resolution (ADR) is a non-judicial method of resolving civil disputes. Rather than filing a lawsuit, the opposing parties agree to allow a neutral third party to hear the dispute. There are a variety of reasons for using ADR:

- The courts in most states are overburdened with cases.
- The costs of civil litigation in terms of both time and money is high.
- Public policy and economic concerns favor ADR over litigation.

ADR is intended as an alternative to the traditional civil litigation process. It's important to remember that, in this process, we don't look for justice; we look to resolve a problem, not win a fight. Some of the more common forms of ADR are discussed below.

Non-Binding Mediation

Many jurisdictions now require both parties to formally mediate a lawsuit before proceeding to trial. Preparing for mediation is much like preparing for trial. Whether the parties willingly submit to mediation or are ordered to do so by the court, mediation should be approached in good faith. This generally means the parties must be willing to settle the case.

Mediation gives both parties an opportunity to present their cases to a neutral person in a less structured forum than a courtroom. Generally, the parties go to mediation after a significant amount of discovery has been completed, and they have had the opportunity to weigh the evidence in the case, including the credibility of the parties and witnesses and the merit of specific evidence.

In order to encourage uninhibited dialogue about the case, all discussions during a mediation session are confidential and can't be disclosed by the mediator or by the parties involved. In addition, information learned about the case can't be used in a trial if mediation fails. Here are some thoughts to remember if you're involved in mediation:

- Never take a position that a case should not be settled unless you are absolutely sure you'll win in court.
- Don't assume that your attorney believes that you committed the acts alleged by the plaintiff, or that you are responsible for the plaintiff s injury and/or damages if your attorney recommends settling the case.
- Mediators make suggestions, and do not make binding decisions.

Binding Arbitration

Unlike mediation, in binding arbitration the decision of the arbitrator is final. There is no appeal, and the case can't be moved into a lawsuit. The fundamental reason for using arbitration is to provide a relatively quick and inexpensive resolution of a dispute by avoiding the expense and delay of court proceedings. Other reasons for using arbitration are that it:

- Provides a means of avoiding the formalities and technicalities of litigation
- Helps avoid congested court dockets
- Is a private proceeding that does not result in a public record
- Submits disputes to recognized experts in the field of disagreement
- Ordinarily produces less open hostility than litigation

A submission to arbitration is usually based on a term of a contract or a requirement of a statute. Submitted issues may be legal, factual, or both. The language of the submission controls the scope of the arbitrator's powers. Doubts with respect to the arbitrability of the subject matter of a dispute are usually resolved in favor of arbitration. After the submission, the arbitrator conducts a hearing. Both parties are allowed to present evidence and to argue their points of view. The decision, known as an award, is issued by the arbitrator. The award does not need to state findings of fact, conclusions of law, or the reasons underlying the decision.

Because the primary objective of arbitration is to avoid the formalities, delay, and expense of litigation, judicial review of an arbitrator's award is extremely limited. The arbitrator's findings of fact and conclusions of law are final and binding.

Mini-Trials

Mini-trials are informal, off-the-record proceedings. Many courts encourage parties to settle their disputes without the need for a long and costly formal trial by holding a mini-trial in which the parties present their evidence and the court decides the outcome. Regardless of the mini-trial outcome, either party is free to proceed to a formal trial if they choose. Mini-trials are most common in family disputes.

PART II

The Process of Litigation

3

Annie's Case

In the pages that follow, we outline a fictitious incident that leads to a lawsuit and subsequent litigation. Our purpose is to allow you to place the elements of a typical lawsuit into context and examine those elements, as they are introduced in "Annie's Case," in Chapters Four through Nine. All names, places, exhibits, and events characterized in this chapter are imaginary and do not reflect any real actions, incidents, persons, or places.

While Annie's case and the events leading to this lawsuit relate directly to a school district's alleged negligence and subsequent questions of liability, the principles of litigation outlined in this and subsequent chapters can be applied to almost all cases, constitutional or non-constitutional, that schools and school leaders commonly experience. In other words, legal procedures are basically the same whether the case is founded, for example, on a personnel or tort issue, a First Amendment right, or a Fourth Amendment question. The breadth of civil law encompasses case law of considerable diversity.

In the case described here, Annie Smith, an eight-year-old third-grader at Red Ridge Elementary School, was injured at school, and her parents have filed suit against the school district. To introduce the case, the following documentation is provided without comment:

1. Letter from the School Board's attorneys

2. Excerpts from the Principal's Interrogatory

3. Copy of the Initial Accident Report

4. Copies of Work Orders

5. The Formal Complaint

6. Plaintiff's Exhibit 1

7. Plaintiff's Exhibit 2

8. Plaintiff's Exhibit 3

After reviewing these documents, you should be able to see the issues that might be raised by the plaintiffs in this case, as well as some of the defense strategies that might be developed. In subsequent chapters, you will be able to apply "Annie's case" to selected elements of the litigation process. (Look for the shaded boxes that occasionally appear in the text.) In Chapter Nine, we'll see how Annie's case is decided, and reveal some additional insights into the case. Normally, when a complaint is filed on behalf of a minor child, the name of the child is not stated in the formal documentation. For the purposes of this book, we felt it would be easier to understand the hypothetical case if we included the names of all of the players.

GREEN, BLACK & WHITE, LLP
ATTORNEYS AT LAW

Rory W. Green, Of Counsel

Albert T. Black

Stephen C. White

Carol J. Montague

MEMO

TO: Board of Education Members, c/o Mr. Steven Broward, Chairperson, School Board, Red Ridge Unified School District No. 435

       Dr. Johnson Clark, Superintendent of Schools, Red Ridge Unified School District No. 435

       Mr. Christopher Williams, Principal, Red Ridge Elementary School

FR: Stephen White

       Chalice Stevens, Legal Assistant

DT: August 23, 2006

RE: Complaint being filed (Smith v. Red Ridge School District No. 435)

Ladies and Gentlemen:

As the law firm and counsel retained by the Red Ridge Unified School District No. 435 Board of Education, it has been brought to our attention by attorneys representing the firm of Wright, Butler, McCanon & Tate that each of you can expect, over the next few weeks, to be served with a formal Complaint brought by Mr. and Mrs. James Smith on behalf of their minor child, Ann Smith. It is our understanding that the Complaint alleges improper actions by representatives of the school district, which may have resulted in injuries to Ann while at Red Ridge Elementary School. We further understand that all of the above-named persons receiving this memo will be named in the pending lawsuit as defendants. We do not have additional details about the Complaint or its allegations at this time. We simply wanted to advise you that we have received this information from pending plaintiff's attorneys, and that you should be prepared to be served. Upon such service, we advise and ask each of you to take the following very important steps:

1)   Contact Chalice Stevens, my assistant, at 642-450-5555 ext. 67, to let her know that you have been served.

2)   Withhold any and all comments about the Complaint or its contents until I can schedule a meeting with each of you. (Board as a group in executive session, Clark and Williams individually)

3)   Refer any and all questions about the Complaint or pending litigation directly to our office.

4)   Please collect and secure any information, i.e., reports, memos, log entries, etc., that you may have in your possession regarding the allegations in the Complaint.

5)   Do not share or discuss any of the allegations with any of your colleagues or employees at this time. Chris, this is especially important for you, as we, and plaintiff's attorneys, will more than likely be seeking witnesses, if any, from your school's faculty and/or staff.

6)   Finally, if any of you have any questions or concerns, please don't hesitate to call me or Chalice immediately.

Excerpts (Lines 11-41, 67-75, 231-239)
from the Interrogatory of
Christopher Layton Williams,
Principal of Red Ridge Elementary School

Question: Describe, in your own words, as best you can, the events surrounding the incident involving Ann Darwin Smith.

Answer:

11. On April 16th, 2006, at approximately 1:10, I was in my office at the

12. school, visiting with the parents of a sixth-grade student about a discipline

13. problem we were experiencing with their son. We had just concluded our

14. conversation when Maria Louise Tinsdale, a teacher's aide, came running

15. into my office. She said that a child had been injured on the playground and

16. that they needed me there right away. I excused myself and quickly

17. followed Ms. Tinsdale to the playground. When I arrived, I saw that teacher

18. Jean Markley was kneeling over Annie Smith, a third-grader in Mrs. Markley's

19. class. Another teacher, Bill Matthews, was supervising the other children on

20. the playground, keeping them away from Annie and Mrs. Markley. Annie

21. was bleeding from a wound on her forehead, and from the position of her

22. leg, I felt pretty sure it was broken. Without a school nurse on duty (itinerate

23. scheduling) to help me determine the extent of Annie's injuries, I sent Ms.

24. Tinsdale back to the building to call 911 for assistance. Fire department

25. paramedics arrived within approximately 7 minutes, and they determined

26.   that Annie probably had multiple injuries and should be transported to the

27. hospital. I concurred, and as soon as they had Annie in the ambulance, I

28. returned to the building and called both of Annie's parents. (Approximately

29. 1:30) I then notified my administrative assistant (Ms. Charlene Lamont) that

30. I was leaving the building, and went directly to the hospital (Wake Center). I

31. met with Mr. and Mrs. Smith and explained, as best I could, that I thought

32. that the swing that Annie was playing on broke and Annie fell. Later, after

33. returning to school, I found out from my custodian, Wilson Reynolds, that a

34. bolt holding one of the swing's chains had broken. He showed me the bolt

35. and I put it in the top drawer of my desk so I could show our district's

36. maintenance department what had happened. I filled out an accident

37. report. That evening, I called the Smith's home to check on Annie and Mr.

38. Smith told me that Annie had "extensive injuries" and would be in the

39. hospital for "a length of time yet to be determined." I went to the hospital

40. the next afternoon to visit Annie and learned that she had broken her arm,

41. knee, and ankle, and had a serious cut on her forehead.

Question: To your best knowledge, when was the last time your playground equipment was inspected?

Answer:

67. All of our playgrounds, kindergarten, primary, and intermediate, are

68. inspected daily by the school's custodian, Mr. Reynolds. If equipment is

69. damaged or broken, he notifies me immediately and we rope off the area,

70. and I submit a district work order for repairs. Since our playgrounds are

71. used extensively by neighborhood children and adults, we often find trash

72. and broken glass that needs to be picked up before our students use the

73. areas. In addition, in July of each school year I've been principal here for

74. three years, I submit a work order to district maintenance to have all of our

75. playground equipment inspected and repaired before school starts.

(Continued)

(Continued)

Question: What was the ratio of students to adult supervisors assigned to the play-ground area at the time of the incident?

Answer:

231.   The incident with Annie took place in the primary grades area of our

232.   playgrounds. At the time of Annie's accident, 3 primary classrooms were at

233.   recess. 2 teachers and a teacher's aide were assigned and on duty for

234.   approximately 82 children. I'm often in the area, but I was in a parent

235.   conference at that time. I require that playground supervisors disperse

236.   themselves around the playground, but I've learned since the incident that

237.   at the time of Annie's accident, all three of them were gathered in one

238.   place. Even though they weren't dispersed, they could see the entire

239.   playground from where they were.

Table 3.1   Copy of the Initial Accident Report

RED RIDGE UNIFIED SCHOOL DISTRICT NO. 435

ACCIDENT REPORTING FORM

Date Reported:	April 16, 2006
Name of School or Department:	Red Ridge Elementary
Reporting Official:	Chris Williams
Date of Accident:	April 16, 2006
Time of Accident:	1:20 p.m.
Type of Injury:	Head wound, possible fractures
Name of Injured Party:	Ann (Annie) Smith, 3rd grader

Deposition of Injured Party:

First aid applied to head wound. Called for paramedics. Covered Annie with blanket. Itinerate nurse was not scheduled to be at Red Ridge Elementary that date. Paramedics took Annie to Wake Center Hospital.

Reporting Official's Comment(s):

Chain or chain fastener on swing set in primary playground area broke. Child was thrown or fell to the ground. Three supervisors were on duty and in the area. Parents were located and advised. Principal's decision to call ambulance. Followed up immediately with trip to the hospital—visited personally with parents of Annie— called their home that evening to follow up.

School Site or Department Copy (Form No. 32-571)

(Send District Copy to: The Office of the
Assistant Superintendent for Personnel and Student Services)

Table 3.2   Copies of School District Work Orders re. Playground
Maintenance Initiated by the Principal During the Years
2003, 2004, 2005

RED RIDGE UNIFIED SCHOOL DISTRICT NO. 435

Building or Grounds Maintenance Request

Date of Request:	July 14, 2005
School or Department:	Red Ridge Elementary School
Requested by:	Chris Williams
Nature of Request:	Please inspect and repair all playground equipment and fences.

School Site or Department Copy (Form No. 22-003)
(Send District Copy to: The Office of the Director of Maintenance)

RED RIDGE UNIFIED SCHOOL DISTRICT NO. 435

Building or Grounds Maintenance Request

Date of Request:	July 18, 2004
School or Department:	Red Ridge Elementary School
Requested by:	Chris Williams
Nature of Request:	Please inspect and repair all playground equipment and fences.

School Site or Department Copy (Form No. 22-003)
(Send District Copy to: The Office of the Director of Maintenance)

RED RIDGE UNIFIED SCHOOL DISTRICT NO. 435

Building or Grounds Maintenance Request

Date of Request:	July 22, 2003
School or Department:	Red Ridge Elementary School
Requested by:	Chris Williams
Nature of Request:	Please inspect and repair all playground equipment and fences.

School Site or Department Copy (Form No. 22-003)
(Send District Copy to: The Office of the Director of Maintenance)

The Complaint

IN THE CIRCUIT COURT FOR BATTLEFIELD COUNTY, VIRGINIA

MARGARET DARWIN SMITH, Individually	)
	)
and	)
	)
JAMES ALLEN SMITH, Individually, and	)
on behalf of their minor child,	)
ANN DARWIN SMITH	)
2339 Highland Court,	)
Red Ridge, Virginia 20941	)
Plaintiffs,	)
v.	)
	)
RED RIDGE UNIFIED SCHOOL DISTRICT NO. 435	) **DOCKET NO.**
	) **06-541-A**
a body corporate,	)
Serve: STEVEN BROWARD	)
Chairperson, School Board, Red Ridge Unified	)
School District No. 435,	)
123 East Market Street,	)
Red Ridge, Virginia 20941,	)
and	)
	)
DR. JOHNSON SEYMOUR CLARK	)
individually and in his official capacity as	)
Superintendent of Schools,	)
Red Ridge Unified School District No. 435,	)
123 East Market Street,	)
Red Ridge, Virginia 20941	)
	)
and	)
	)
CHRISTOPHER LAYTON WILLIAMS	)
individually and in his official capacity as Principal,	)
Red Ridge Elementary School	)
4067 West Slope Avenue	)
Red Ridge, Virginia 20901	)
	)
Defendants	)

COMPLAINT

JURISDICTION

1. This Court has jurisdiction pursuant to Annotated Code of Virginia, Courts and Judicial Proceedings, Sections 1-542 and 6-114.

(Continued)

(Continued)

PARTIES

2. Plaintiff, Margaret Darwin Smith is an adult resident of Battlefield County, Red Ridge, Virginia, and is the mother of the minor child, Ann Darwin Smith.

3. Plaintiff, James Allen Smith is an adult resident of Battlefield County, Red Ridge, Virginia, and is the father of the minor child, Ann Darwin Smith.

4. Plaintiff, Ann Darwin Smith (hereafter "Annie"), at all times relevant herein, was and is below the majority age and is under the care and custody of her parents, James and Margaret Smith. At all times relevant herein, she resided with her parents at their home located at 2339 Highland Court, Red Ridge, Virginia 20941.

5. Defendant, Red Ridge Unified School District No. 435 School Board ("RRSB") is a body corporate established pursuant to Va. Code §24.1-69. At all times pertinent hereto, RRSB employed the Defendants Clark and Williams and was responsible for all other personnel, equipment, and buildings and grounds that are part of Red Ridge Unified School District No. 435.

6. Defendant, Dr. Johnson Seymour Clark ("Clark") was, at all times pertinent hereto, an employee of RRSB, employed as superintendent of schools with administrative and supervisory control over Defendant Williams, as well as administrative and supervisory control over all other personnel, equipment, and buildings and grounds that are part of Red Ridge Unified School District No. 435.

7. Defendant, Christopher Layton Williams ("Williams") was, at all times pertinent hereto, an employee of RRSB, employed as the principal at Red Ridge Elementary School with administrative and supervisory control over all adult personnel, all students enrolled at the school, as well as administrative and supervisory control over all equipment, buildings and grounds that are part of Red Ridge Elementary School.

FACTUAL SUMMARY

8. Annie was, at the time of this incident, an eight-year-old, third-grade student at Red Ridge Elementary School.

9. Annie was, at the time of this incident, an above average student in good physical condition.

10. On April 16th, 2006, at approximately 1:30 p.m. Annie's parents received individual telephone calls from Annie's school principal Williams notifying them that Annie had been involved in an accident at Red Ridge Elementary school and, on the advice of Williams, was being transported to the emergency room at Wake Center Hospital.

11. On April 16th, 2006, at approximately 2:00 p.m. Williams met Annie's parents, Margaret and James Smith, at Wake Center Hospital and explained to them that Annie had been injured when a chain holding a swing she had been playing on broke, sending Annie to the ground.

12. Annie's injuries, as a result of the fall, consisted of fractures to her right arm, left knee, and right ankle. In addition, Annie sustained a deep-scarring laceration to her forehead believed to have been caused by the approximately 12-foot fall and impact of the broken length of ¾-inch swing chain.

13. On April 16th, at approximately 8:15 p.m., Williams telephoned the Smith's home to check on the Annie's condition. At that time he talked with Annie's father and disclosed that the school's custodian had found the cause of Annie's fall. A 3-inch bolt holding one of the swing set's chains to the top rail of the swing had worn and broken in half.

14. The actions and/or inactions of the RRSB and its employees have caused significant physical and emotional harm to Annie, tremendous emotional strain on her parents, and significant financial impact and harm to the entire family.

15. The actions and/or inactions of the RRSB and its employees caused Annie to miss the final weeks of her third-grade school year and the long-awaited "fly-up" ceremony for primary students to the intermediate level, adding additional significant harm to Annie's emotional well-being.

16. In all material respects, the RRSB, the administration of the school district, and its managers and supervisors have failed to properly supervise and train their employees, and allowed this incident to occur.

CAUSES OF ACTION

COUNT I
(Defendants RRSB *et al.*)
(Negligence)

17. Plaintiffs reallege and incorporate by reference paragraphs 1 through 16.

18. Defendants RRSB, Clark, and Williams committed various acts that fell below the reasonable standard of care for an individual similarly situated. These acts include, but are not limited to, the improper supervision of minor children while on the playground and the improper inspection and maintenance of equipment used by minor children who are unable, by the nature of their age and experience level, to foresee certain dangerous instrumentalities.

(Continued)

(Continued)

COUNT II
(Defendants RRSB *et al.*)
(Improper Maintenance)

19. Plaintiffs reallege and incorporate by reference paragraphs 1 through 18.

20. Defendants RRSB, Clark, and Williams committed various acts that fell below the reasonable standard of care for an individual similarly situated. These acts include, but are not limited to, their failure to provide proper inspection and maintenance of playground equipment that is provided expressly for the use of young children at the school during official school hours.

COUNT III
(Defendants RRSB *et al.*)
(Improper Supervision)

21. Plaintiffs reallege and incorporate by reference paragraphs 1 through 20.

22. Defendants RRSB, Clark, and Williams committed various acts that fell below the reasonable standard of care for an individual similarly situated. These acts include, but are not limited to, their failure to properly supervise young children during recess and while at play on the school's playground(s).

COUNT IV
(Defendants RRSB *et al.*)
(Breach of Obligation to Provide a Safe Place)
(Duty and Standard of Care)

23. Plaintiffs reallege and incorporate by reference paragraphs 1 through 22.

24. Defendants RRSB, Clark, and Williams committed various acts that fell below the reasonable standard of care for an individual similarly situated. Contrary to providing Annie with a safe and appropriate setting, the school district, through its employees, knowingly, through their actions and/or inactions, placed Annie in a position clearly contrary to the setting, educational, and emotional experiences expected in a public elementary school.

WHEREFORE, plaintiffs James Smith and Margaret Smith individually and on behalf of Ann Smith demand damages against the defendants as follows:

(A) from defendant Williams, compensatory damages in the amount of $20,000 and punitive damages in the amount of $100,000;

(B) from defendant Clark, compensatory damages in the amount of $20,000 and punitive damages in the amount of $100,000;

(C)   from defendant RRSB, compensatory damages in the amount of $20,000 and punitive damages in the amount of $1,000,000;

(D)   from all defendants, the cost of this litigation, including attorney's fees; and

(E)   such other relief as the court deems just and proper.

PLAINTIFFS DEMAND TRIAL BY JURY.

<u>VERIFICATION</u>

WE HAVE REVIEWED THE ALLEGATIONS AND FACTS ABOVE AND FIND THEM TRUE AND CORRECT TO THE BEST OF OUR INFORMATION, KNOWLEDGE AND BELIEF.

James A. Smith
James A Smith

Margaret D. Smith
Margaret D. Smith

Respectfully submitted for,

Wright, Butler, McCanon & Tate by

Graham D. Sterling
Graham D. Sterling, Esq.
5336 Pewter Path
Suite 2
Red Ridge, Virginia 20941

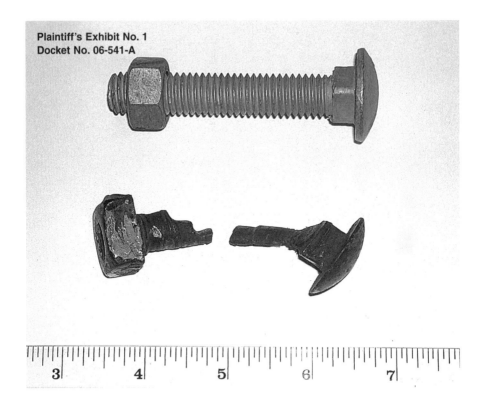

Plaintiff's Exhibit No. 1
Docket No. 06-541-A

Plaintiff's Exhibit No. 2
Docket No. 06-541-A

Plaintiff's Exhibit No. 3
Docket No. 06-541-A

Distance from primary area swing set to school building where supervisors were congregated = 87.3 yards

4

The Litigation Process

In a criminal trial, a government entity (federal, state, or county) prosecutes individuals or organizations who have been charged with criminal acts. In civil litigation, a private individual or organization (the plaintiff or petitioner) sues another private individual or organization (the defendant or respondent) for a declaration of rights, or to obtain a remedy for an alleged wrong. Civil litigation is primarily compensatory because the plaintiff's usual objective is a monetary judgment for losses caused by injury to a legally recognized interest. In contrast, criminal proceedings are primarily punitive as the prosecution's objectives are punishment and deterrence. In a civil action, the plaintiff seeks to force the defendant either to act or to refrain from acting in a specified manner, or to pay monetary damages as a result of a prior commission of an act, or the omission of an act.

Civil Litigation

Civil litigation is a court-directed proceeding that applies a body of procedural law designed to assure that both the plaintiff's and the defendant's individual views of the facts and relevant law are presented and weighed equitably. The plaintiff and the defendant (through their attorneys) present conflicting positions of fact or law to an impartial judge and/or a jury. The two primary types of civil proceedings are lawsuits involving contracts and lawsuits involving torts. In a civil suit in which a contract is at issue, one party alleges that another party breached an enforceable promise. In a civil suit in which a tort (a negligent wrong) is at issue, one party alleges that another party breached a legal duty that arises from society's (not private) expectations of acceptable conduct, and that the breach caused injury to the plaintiff's person or property. The defendant is allegedly responsible for a wrongful act (action) or for a failure to act (inaction where action was called for).

> **Case Study Reference #1:**
>
> In Annie's case, the plaintiffs alleged that the defendants were responsible for a "failure to act" (inaction where action is called for) in properly maintaining equipment and properly supervising the playground where Annie was injured.

The litigation process consists of proceedings in which the opposing parties seek to persuade the decision-maker (judge or jury/triers of fact) that their respective views of the law or the facts are legitimate and, as a result, they should be entitled to prevail. The civil litigation process described below varies from jurisdiction to jurisdiction across the country, but it will generally follow the pattern we describe here.

The Pleading or Complaint

A lawsuit begins with the plaintiff filing a Complaint in a state court or federal district court. The nature of the causes of action or claims claimed in the lawsuit determines whether the case will be heard in state or federal court. A Complaint has several sections:

Style or Caption

Jurisdiction and Venue

Parties

Background Facts

Causes of Action

Relief or Remedies Sought

The sections regarding the court's "Jurisdiction" and "Venue" are simply procedural. Generally, the "Style," "Parties," "Background Facts," "Causes of Action" and "Relief and Remedies" sections are the "hot buttons" of interest to us as defendants. So, let's concentrate on them first.

The "Style" or "Caption" (the block on the first page of the Complaint) identifies the name of the plaintiff(s); the school district et al. (this includes you) as the defendant(s); the state or federal district court in which the lawsuit is filed, and the case number.

The "Parties" section generally identifies the individuals who are suing and being sued. The section normally states whether the defendant is being sued in his or her individual capacity and/or official capacity, if the defendant works for a governmental entity, i.e. a school district.

Individual Capacity

A person may be found to be personally liable if he or she acts outside the course and scope of his or her duties. A defendant sued in his or her individual capacity may be personally responsible for paying a money judgment that exceeds insurance or other indemnification coverage.

Official Capacity

An employee-defendant sued in his or her official capacity is not personally responsible for any portion of a judgment. Again, this capacity in which an individual is sued is applicable only to public employees.

The "Background Facts" section of the Complaint generally contains the "who, what, when, where, how, and why" of the lawsuit. This is the plaintiff's version of the incident or occurrence on which the lawsuit is based and may or may not be accurate as far as you're concerned. Nevertheless, it provides insight into what the plaintiff believes happened and how he or she feels about you, your school, your district, or the manner in which he or she was treated.

A "Cause of Action" is the statute, common law, or constitutional provision on which the plaintiff bases a claim for relief or remedies. (Note: Occasionally the "Background Facts" and "Cause of Action" sections are combined.) The plaintiff may amend this section of the Complaint to include additional causes of action during the course of a lawsuit. Normally, however, such an amendment must be filed at least seven days before trial in a state court. In federal court, the deadline for amending the Cause of Action is established by the presiding judge.

The "Relief or Remedies Sought" section of the Complaint identifies the amount of damages and other relief, such as reinstatement or other injunctive relief, sought. The dollar amount stated in the Complaint very often has no relationship to the amount of harm the plaintiff actually suffered or to the amount of money he or she expects to recover if the plaintiff's lawsuit is successful.

The Summons

The summons is the official notification that an individual has been sued. It is part of the "Service of Process." The Service of Process is the official act by a plaintiff that notifies an individual that he or she has been sued. The summons may be personally served to the defendant, or it may be constructively served by registered mail or physical posting at his or her residence. In the summons, the defendant is advised that, if no action is taken within the specified period of time, the plaintiff may win the case by default. A judgment by default means that the plaintiff receives what he or she requested the court to grant without further proceedings. The deadline for responding to a Complaint begins running upon receipt of service.

The Response

Generally, a defendant must respond to a Complaint no later than 30 days after receipt of the summons. The response may be in the form of an answer or another form of responsive pleading.

The Answer

In many states, if the lawsuit is filed in state court, the answer may be nothing more than a general denial of all the allegations in the Complaint. If the lawsuit is filed in federal court, the answer must specifically admit or deny the allegations made in the Complaint. The answer must also identify any affirmative defenses that the defendant intends to raise. The answer may contain counterclaims against the plaintiff. A counterclaim declares an independent cause of action by the defendant against the plaintiff. The purpose of a counterclaim is either to oppose or to offset the plaintiff's claim.

Case Study Reference #2:

In Annie's case, the defendants' responses were a general denial of all allegations in the Complaint. The defendants contended they were not negligent, and that Annie's injuries were an unavoidable accident. The defendants didn't file a counter claim

Other Responses

Regardless of the jurisdiction in which the lawsuit is filed or whether an answer is filed, the first several weeks after a summons are generally used to file various pleadings or motions and to schedule hearings in which the defense will try to refute or mitigate the Complaint. The goal of the pleadings and/or motions is to have the case dismissed without further action or to lay the foundation for dismissal. Three common responsive pleadings filed in state courts are the Demurrer, the Motion to Strike, and the Motion to Dismiss.

The Demurrer is a responsive pleading that seeks a judgment for the defendant based on defects appearing on the face of the Complaint. In other words, does the plaintiff have legal grounds for a lawsuit, even if all the facts, as stated in the Complaint, are true? A Motion to Strike is a pleading filed by the defendant asking the Court to strike portions of the Complaint based on legal defects in the wording. A Motion to Dismiss is a pleading filed by the defendant, prior to trial, that, if granted, will eliminate all or some of a plaintiff s claims. If all claims are eliminated, the case is dismissed with or without prejudice. If dismissed with prejudice, the claims may not be refiled. If dismissed without prejudice, the claims may be refiled.

> **Case Study Reference #3:**
>
> In Annie's case, no pretrial motions were made by the defendants. The plaintiffs had clear legal standing and grounds for a lawsuit.

The Discovery Process

To prepare for trial and to encourage settlements prior to trial, each party has the right to learn as much as possible about the adversary's case before trial. This is called the discovery process. The purpose of discovery is to assist the parties in determining what the evidence may consist of, who the potential witnesses are, and what specific issues may be relevant. Discovery also helps to maintain pertinent evidence that might otherwise be lost. An effective discovery process prevents unexpected evidence at trial and ensures that both parties have time to fashion the most effective counterarguments.

Discovery not only assists the parties in preparing their arguments, but also narrows the issues to be resolved. One rationale for permitting the parties to learn as much as they can about both sides of the case is to encourage early settlement. It is estimated that 90% of all controversies never reach the trial stage, leaving only 10% of the disputes to be resolved in court. In addition, the information obtained through discovery may often be so compelling that either party may successfully move for summary judgment and avoid the trial.

In all jurisdictions, the scope of discovery in civil litigation is comprehensive. Information is discoverable if it is relevant to the factual circumstances out of which the lawsuit arose, is not part of the attorney's work product, and is not subject to another testimonial privilege. For example, communication between an attorney and his or her client that is meant to be confidential is neither discoverable nor admissible at trial.

Although the legal limits of discovery are set by statute and overseen by the trial judge, the actual discovery process is conducted by attorneys, not the court. The discovery process is an important part of litigation procedures and, as a result, can consume days, weeks, or months.

The discovery process may include several steps. Initial Disclosure is required in most federal district courts. The parties involved are generally required to exchange documents that may have some bearing on the claims and defenses raised in the initial pleadings, and to identify individuals with knowledge of facts relevant to the case.

Informal discovery is merely the defendant's and plaintiff's attorneys talking to friendly or non-hostile witnesses who may have information about the case and obtaining documents that have a bearing on their client's claims or possible defenses in the case.

Formal discovery is the process for obtaining information about the case from the opposing party. This includes requests to admit certain facts. There are four commonly used formal procedures for obtaining information from the opposing party.

Interrogatories

Interrogatories are written questions asking for information about certain incidents, occurrences, positions taken by the party, policies, procedures, etc. The answers provided to these questions can be used as evidence at trial.

Request for Production

Either party can request certain documents that he or she believes are relevant or will lead to the discovery of admissible evidence. The documents requested may include such items as copies of e-mail, personnel files, computer disks, medical records, education records, income tax returns, and other financial documents. It is important that, as a defendant, you provide your attorneys with all such documents in your possession, custody, or control that may have a bearing on the claims or your defense. You generally must provide the documents no later than 30 days after receipt of the request. State and federal "Rules of Civil

---

Case Study Reference #4:

In Annie's case, the defendants identified four persons not named in the Complaint who had "a knowledge of facts" relevant to the case. They were:

Red Ridge Elementary School Teacher, Jean Markley

Red Ridge Elementary School Teacher, William (Bill) Matthews

Red Ridge Elementary School Teacher Aide, Maria Louise Tinsdale

Red Ridge Elementary School Head Custodian, Wilson Reynolds

The defendants provided individual contact information that will also be included for all identified persons.

Procedure" require the parties to supplement responses. If the documents are not provided to the opposing party, they can't be used on your behalf as evidence during the trial.

Requests for Admission

Requests for Admission are requests for a party to admit or deny specific facts alleged by the opposing party. Requests for admission are often used to limit the issues in a case and/or to discover a party's true position on a specific issue.

Depositions

Depositions are formal direct question and answer sessions conducted by the opposing attorney. At a deposition, the opposing attorney is allowed to ask the deponent questions about the case while the deponent is under oath. The questions and answers are recorded by a court reporter and transcribed for use during the litigation. The deposition can also be videotaped. The testimony provided during the deposition can be used as evidence at trial, or for any matter related to the litigation.

The deposition may be the most important pretrial event of the case. Often, case strategy, and ultimately case resolution, is dictated by the deponent's performance and ability to handle questioning by the opposing attorney(s). Deposition questions are prepared by opposing attorneys. Remember that, in both depositions and interrogatories, if your testimony (or anyone else's connected with the case) at trial is inconsistent with what you or they stated in either a deposition or interrogatory, it can lead to the impeachment of your or their credibility as a witness. The deposition process should be viewed as three separate events:

Deposition Preparation

Preparation for a deposition is as important as the deposition itself. It is imperative that you be readily available to thoroughly prepare for the deposition. Preparation includes reviewing the facts of the case, reviewing all relevant documents, familiarizing yourself with the deposition process, and discussing with your attorney how to handle troublesome issues and aggressive plaintiff's attorneys.

Testimony During the Deposition

The opposing attorney(s) will have the opportunity to inquire into a broad range of subjects, including, but not limited to, questions about the incident that is the basis of the lawsuit, your personal life, and your personal assets (if you're being sued in an individual capacity). The questions do not need to be relevant to the litigation as long as they are reasonably anticipated to lead to admissible evidence. You should remember three important rules when testifying at a deposition: (1) tell the truth; (2) answer only the questions asked; and (3) don't volunteer information.

No judge is present at the deposition. Therefore, objections made during the testimony are made only for the record and will be ruled upon at the time of trial or at a meeting with the judge. Attorneys may only object to the form of the question, to the responsiveness of the answer, or when the question calls for information protected by a recognized privilege. If the question seeks privileged or confidential information, the attorney(s) will object and advise you not to answer.

Post-Deposition

After the deposition is completed, the defendant has an opportunity to review and sign the document. By signing, the deponent verifies that the deposition transcript correctly reflects the answers he or she gave. You should keep a copy of your deposition and any changes for your personal records and study prior to litigation. Deposition testimony may be used in other proceedings.

A Motion for Summary Judgment is a pleading filed by the defendant, generally at the conclusion of discovery, that seeks a judicial determination of the merits of a claim or claims. If the Motion for Summary Judgment is granted on all of the claims, the case is dismissed and judgment is final. If granted on only some of the claims, the case will proceed on the remaining claim or claims.

In most states, the courts conduct a pretrial conference, a meeting of the judge and all attorneys, for all civil suits. A pretrial conference can be either mandatory or discretionary. The pretrial conference serves two primary purposes:

To shorten the trial by refining or narrowing the issues, or setting guidelines concerning admissibility of evidence and qualifications of witnesses.

To encourage a settlement. If no settlement can be agreed upon, the judge sets a date for the trial. Absent a settlement, the judge will enter an order (the pretrial order) containing all of the amendments to the pleadings, stipulations regarding the facts, and other matters agreed to in the pretrial conference. This pretrial order guides courtroom procedures during the trial. For example, witnesses not listed and approved at the pretrial conference will generally not be allowed to testify.

The Trial

Not all lawsuits make their way to trial. Some are voluntarily or involuntarily dismissed while others are settled. The circumstances surrounding any given case, and the differing approaches of the attorneys involved, make it difficult to predict an outcome. However, if a case reaches the trial stage, the time, energy, and resources spent preparing for the trial increases dramatically.

We are all generally familiar with the various stages of a trial, even if we don't know the precise terms for them. Briefly, the major stages are:

- *Voir dire* or jury selection
- Opening statements by both parties
- Presentation of the plaintiff's case-in-chief
- Motion for Judgment as a Matter of Law or Motion for Instructed Verdict
- Presentation of the defendant's case-in-chief
- Plaintiff's rebuttal
- Another Motion for Judgment as a Matter of Law or Motion for Instructed Verdict
- Closing arguments by both parties
- The judge's charge (instructions) to the jury
- Jury verdict

Post Trial

The events that follow the conclusion of the trial are solely dependent upon which party prevails and the amount and effect of any judgment against them. Either party can appeal an adverse judgment.

If the plaintiff prevails, he or she may be entitled to attorney's fees and court costs in addition to any monetary judgment or injunctive relief. If monetary damages are awarded, the plaintiff may introduce post-judgment discovery in an effort to ascertain the amount and location of a defendant's assets.

Appeal

If there were legal errors at trial, or there was insufficient evidence to support the verdict, the losing party may be entitled to appeal the result. Civil cases tried to a verdict are seldom reversed.

Other Civil Litigation Procedures

The following are brief explanations of other common elements of civil litigation. For each definition, there are extensions and/or exceptions that may or may not come into play and have an effect on a lawsuit and the parties involved.

Cause of Action

An injury of one person by another does not necessarily give the victim a cause of action. Courts generally don't act without a genuine dispute. A cause of action is a claim, in law and fact, sufficient to demand judicial attention. It is the right by which a party may institute a judicial proceeding.

- This right can belong to a particular person or class of persons.
- The person is said to "have standing" to institute judicial proceedings.
- A wrongful act (commission or omission) by another triggers the right to assert a claim.
- A cause of action is said to accrue or to exist at the moment when the injury occurs. This is important because of statutes of limitations.
- The plaintiff must demonstrate a cause of action (a claim sufficient to demand judicial attention, the basis for the lawsuit) in the Complaint. If the Complaint fails to state a proper cause of action, it will be dismissed.

Parties to Civil Litigation

The party who initiates a civil lawsuit is the plaintiff. The party who is sued is the defendant. The plaintiff initiates a lawsuit by filing a formal Complaint to the court stating the cause of action. The Complaint must contain sufficient facts to inform the court and the defendant of the nature of the plaintiff's cause of action.

If the result at the trial level is appealed, the party appealing is usually referred to as the appellant, and the successful party who opposed him or her at the trial court level is called the appellee.

Statute of Limitations

A statute of limitations is a law that fixes the time within which parties must initiate judicial action to enforce rights. Thereafter, they are barred from bringing suit. A statute of limitations codifies the common-law doctrine of *laches,* which bars a claim if undue delay in asserting it would result in prejudice to the other party. Statutes of limitations apply to most actions at law, civil or criminal. A statute of limitations requires a person to file suit in a timely manner, typically within a specified number of years, depending upon the type of lawsuit filed. A plaintiff who waits too long to sue after he or she is wronged loses the right to assert a claim, even if it is clearly meritorious.

A statute of limitations does not require that a lawsuit be completed prior to the expiration of the statutory period. All that is necessary is that the suit be commenced (the Complaint filed) before this period ends.

Standing

A person must have standing to sue in order to maintain, or participate in, a lawsuit. A legal question that arises in every civil lawsuit is whether a litigant is entitled to have the court decide the dispute. To determine whether a potential plaintiff has standing, the court will determine whether:

- The participant can allege a case or controversy.
- The participant has a direct and personal stake in the outcome of the litigation.

Courts have the power and duty to hear only an actual controversy. The parties must have actual interests and competing claims. Such a controversy is said to be capable of being tried in a court of law (justiciable).

Summary Judgment

During the pleadings, and at any time prior to the verdict, either party to the lawsuit may move for summary judgment. In filing a pretrial motion for summary judgment, a party argues that, based on the pleadings or discovery, the party that files the motion is entitled to a judgment under the law. In other words, the evidence produced by discovery is so clear that the party that files the motion is legally entitled to prevail, and a trial is not warranted because there is no genuine issue as to any material fact. In determining its response to the motion, the court views the evidence in the light most favorable to the opposing party. If evidence may be interpreted in two ways, one supporting the motion and the other contradicting it, the motion for summary judgment will most likely be denied. If a judge grants a motion for summary judgment, the losing party may appeal to a higher court.

Jurisdiction and Venue

Jurisdiction is the power of a court to hear a case and render an enforceable decision. Without proper jurisdiction, a court's judgment is void. The venue of a lawsuit is the location of the proceedings. The issue is geographical: Which court is reasonably convenient for the trial? Venue may be proper in more than one place, provided that jurisdiction can be established. In state courts, a typical question is which county in the state is the proper venue. In federal practice, the issue is which United States District Court is proper. Jurisdiction addresses the authority of a court to exercise judicial power. Venue addresses the choice of the place, within a court system having jurisdiction, in which that power should be exercised. The parties' right to have the action brought and heard in a convenient forum is the decisive factor in the venue decision.

> **Case Study Reference #5**
>
> In Annie's case, the plaintiff's attorney moved for a summary judgment. However, the defendant's attorney uncovered, during the discovery process, enough counter-evidence that the judge ruled that a full trial was warranted to prove that the RRSB et al. were not negligent in any actions or inactions.

Class Action

A class action suit is one brought, or defended, by one or more persons representing a large group of similarly situated persons who have been injured by the same defendant, or who may be liable to the same plaintiff. The number of persons in a class is frequently very large, and the suit often involves matters in which no one member of the class would have a sufficient financial interest to warrant litigation; however, combining the interests of all members of the class makes litigation feasible.

Under federal and most state law, one or more members of a class may sue or be sued as representatives of a class provided that:

- The class is so numerous that joinder (the uniting of several causes of action or parties in a single suit) of all members of the class is practicable.
- Questions of law and fact are common to all members of the class.

- Claims or defenses of the representative parties are typical of the entire class.
- Representative parties will fairly and adequately protect the interests of the class.

Criminal Prosecution

While the major objective of civil law is individual compensation, the major objective of criminal law is deterrence and punishment. We all understand that there are many terrible things that may happen to children or adults on school property that are not crimes. However, a single event may result in criminal prosecution, a civil suit, and a district or building-level investigation. For example, in the case of an allegation that a teacher assaulted a student, as a school administrator, you may be forced to juggle the involvement of the police on the criminal side, the attorney for the alleged victim on the civil side, and school district's own investigation process. If the case in which you are involved becomes a criminal case, it will be out of your hands, although you may still be called upon to testify. This section provides, for your information, a brief overview of the events generally associated with the criminal prosecution process.

Criminal law

Criminal law (penal law) is the body of law that controls government sanctions (such as imprisonment and/or fines) as punishment for crimes against the social order. The state becomes involved because the alleged perpetrator has harmed the state by violating a criminal law—committing a crime against the state. Consequently, government officials (federal, state, or county) are responsible for prosecuting criminal offenders.

When a Crime Occurs

If you believe a crime has occurred, either on school property or involving a student, you need to immediately contact the police agency with jurisdiction in the area in which the crime was allegedly committed. The county or city attorney can't charge a person with a crime until he or she receives a referral from a police agency. The county attorney's office doesn't initially investigate crimes; it relies on the police agency with jurisdiction to conduct the investigation. When the police have completed their investigation, and determined that a crime has been committed, they refer the case to the county or city attorney. At that point, the case is logged in and assigned to an individual prosecuting attorney. The case is then reviewed to determine if there is enough evidence to prosecute the alleged perpetrator with a crime.

The first thing a county or city attorney must do is review the police reports to confirm that a crime has been committed, that it took place within the appropriate jurisdiction, and that there is sufficient evidence to prosecute the alleged wrongdoer. When the county or city attorney reviews the case to determine whether or not to prosecute the case, he or she generally asks five questions:

1. Do we have jurisdiction in this case?

2. Do the facts indicate a crime has been committed?

3. Do we know who committed the crime?

4. Is there sufficient evidence to prove the case?

5. Can we afford to prosecute the case? This fifth item must be understood in light of the limited annual budget that a city or county attorney has at his or her disposal.

The Criminal Court Process

There are a number of possible outcomes of a criminal case or charge. The case may be deferred, resulting in a dismissal of the charge if the person successfully completes a deferred prosecution agreement, or may proceed to trial and sentencing. A person can be sentenced only if convicted. A person can be convicted only on his or her plea of guilty, or by a finding of guilt after a trial before a judge or jury. The array of sentencing possibilities is set by state law and ranges from probation to fines to imprisonment.

You may be interested to know that most criminal cases don't go to trial, but are settled by a process of negotiation between the prosecutor and the defendant, generally called plea bargaining. In a plea bargain, the defendant may, in return for a plea of guilty, receive a reduced fine or prison term. All plea agreements must be presented to, and approved by, a judge.

Felony Court Procedure

Felony is the term for a "very serious" crime; misdemeanors are considered to be less serious. In many jurisdictions, a felony is any offence carrying a potential penalty of more than one year in prison. Examples of crimes that are commonly considered to be felonies include aggravated assault, arson, burglary, murder, rape, fraud, embezzlement, etc. The criminal prosecution process described below varies from jurisdiction to jurisdiction across the country, but generally includes:

Initial Appearance: The initial appearance refers to the defendant's first appearance in court, at which time the defendant is informed of the charges and penalties, bail is set, and a date for the preliminary hearing is set.

Preliminary Hearing: At the preliminary hearing, a judge hears testimony to decide if the court has probable cause to believe a crime was committed, and the defendant committed it. If the judge feels there is enough evidence to make the defendant stand trial, the case continues and is "bound over" for trial.

Arraignment: At the arraignment, the defendant enters a plea of guilty, not guilty, or no contest. If the defendant pleads not guilty, a date is set for trial proceedings to begin. If the plea is guilty or no contest, the court sets a date for the sentencing hearing.

Motions: A motion is a formal verbal or written request that asks the judge to decide a legal question brought forward by either the prosecutor or defense attorney before, during, or after the trial.

In Person Status Conference: This conference is a court hearing, held so that the parties can discuss whether an agreement can be reached before the trial date. If an agreement is reached, this conference can become a plea and sentencing hearing.

Trial: A trial is an official hearing in which either a jury (in a jury trial) or judge (in a bench trial) hears the facts of the case. Through physical evidence and testimony by witnesses, the prosecutor attempts to prove, beyond reasonable doubt, the defendant's guilt. The defendant has the right to provide evidence in his or her defense to refute the case made by the prosecution. If the defendant is found guilty, the judge may sentence the defendant immediately, or set the date for a sentencing hearing.

Sentencing: In a sentencing hearing, the judge decides how to punish and rehabilitate the defendant. A sentencing hearing follows a plea of guilty or no contest, or a finding of guilty by a jury or judge.

The litigation processes described in this chapter are "business as usual" to practicing attorneys. For them, the processes are relatively simple to follow, understand, and navigate with comfort. For us professional educators, the processes are new, time-consuming, daunting, and difficult to grasp. Our best advice, having experienced the litigation process first hand, is that you look at litigation in a "Renaissance Man" frame of mind—as an interesting learning experience.

5

Working With an Attorney: Attorneys' Considerations in Deciding Whether to Accept a Case and Bring a Lawsuit

The decision to initiate litigation is typically made by litigants (potential plaintiffs) in consultation with their legal advisors (attorneys). The first step in a civil lawsuit begins long before a case is even filed, with what is commonly called pre-suit preparation. In this situation, a potential plaintiff contacts an attorney and describes what happened to him or her, or a member of his or her family. This is when the attorney determines whether the case has merit, and whether he or she is going to agree to accept the case.

Pre-suit preparation often includes requests for records, interviews with potential witnesses, and a general investigation, by the lawyer, of the potential plaintiff's claim. The primary purpose of the pre-suit stage is for the attorney to determine (1) whether a case exists, (2) what theory of liability exists, and (3) what the potential damages may be.

Two major elements impact the decision-making process. The first is the likelihood of success, in terms of both whether the desired decision can be realized and whether the decision will be enforceable. The second is the means to finance the litigation.

When the potential litigant must directly finance the proposed litigation, the decision to proceed rests almost entirely with the potential litigant. Attorneys may seek to dissuade potential litigants from pursuing their grievance, citing such factors as the financial, time, and emotional costs, as well as the uncertainty inherent in the process. If the potential litigant has the financial backing of a third party (i.e. litigation expense insurance, legal aid, or a union), the third party will typically be actively involved in the decision to proceed or not to proceed. As potential defendants in all kinds of litigation, and as employees of school districts, we are insured, and as a result, our district's insurance carrier becomes both the third party and the effective defendant.

Before an attorney takes a case, he or she will carefully review the facts of the potential client's case, and weigh a number of factors to determine the potential strength of the client's claims and the likelihood of success. Here are some of the factors that, at a minimum, will be examined and discussed:

- The precise nature of the potential plaintiff's claim
- The probable measure of damages or other relief
- The plaintiff's objective, e.g., money, respect, revenge, political motives, etc.
- The plaintiff's reasonableness, e.g., fair settlement vs. "I want the school district to suffer."
- The evidence available to prove the plaintiff's claim, and the additional evidence still needed
- The difficulty and likelihood of gathering additional pertinent information that can be considered as evidence
- The cost of seeking and finding additional information and evidence, preparing the case, and conducting a trial
- Whether the plaintiff is likely to "stay the course," or change his or her mind, and abandon the claim as no longer worth the time and effort to pursue, after the lawyer has invested time, talent, and resources
- How believable the plaintiff is

- Who the probable defendant is
- How believable the defendant might be if a trial ensues
- Whether the defendant, or allies, might have any possible claims against the plaintiff
- The importance of the case as "precedent"
- The relative effect of possible adverse publicity for both the plaintiff and the defendant
- What the defendant typically does when sued
- In contingency fee cases, whether the adversary is likely to pay the judgment if the plaintiff is successful
- Whether there may be a "deep pocket" defendant who has responsibility for some or all of the claim
- In non-contingency cases, if the client is the plaintiff, whether he or she will be able to pay the fees and expenses of the litigation
- The possibility of an informal settlement on reasonable terms
- The court the claim could be heard in, how long it would take to go to trial, and the quality and attitude of its judges
- Whether it makes sense to use alternative dispute resolution techniques (mediation or arbitration) to resolve the argument

Good attorneys are likely to explore these factors, at a minimum, with potential clients, before deciding whether to accept a case. They will also introduce potential clients to the conceptual foundation of our judicial system—that the ritual of due process in litigation and trials is intended to provide a level playing field for both the plaintiffs and the defendants.

Developing a Defense Strategy

A defense strategy typically develops as your attorney gains knowledge of your claims and supporting evidence versus the plaintiff's claims and evidence, and your version of the events versus what he or she knows about the plaintiff's version of the same events.

Case Study Reference #6

In Annie's case, the plaintiffs, the Smith family on behalf of Annie, had a strong and reasonable cause for legal action. Evidence of improper maintenance seemed to be apparent, and there seemed to be a clear question concerning proper supervision of maintenance employees by the RRSB and superintendent, as well as the appropriateness of playground supervision at Annie's school. It looked like a solid, winnable case.

The attorneys for the school board automatically became the attorneys for all of the named defendants.

The process of developing a defense strategy varies from case to case, and is subject to frequent change, as your attorney gradually gains more and more factual information about the events or situations. In other words, your attorney's strategy will probably remain fluid and tentative throughout the discovery process. It's up to you and your attorney, working as a team, to develop the most legally helpful and accurate version of the events or situations appropriate to your case. The result should have characteristics that:

Are consistent with objectively verifiable evidence

Convincingly explain why and how the events in question took place

Have strong potential for gaining the sympathy of a judge or jury.

When developing a defense strategy, your attorney will also consider such factors as:

The reliability of the defense's and plaintiff's witnesses

The local community's attitudes and values

The moral culpability of all parties involved.

Your attorney uses such factors to develop a "theory of the case" that is consistent with provable facts and explains events in a way that is favorable to your side of the issue.

While your attorney's final defense strategy may differ considerably from the defense you favor, the final defense strategy is an outgrowth of your mutual ability to piece together a version of the events that is both truthful and factual, and most likely to produce a satisfactory defense outcome—a verdict of not guilty, or better yet, a motion to dismiss. Remember that, in the final analysis, what the trial strategy is will be determined solely by your attorney. At the same time, the plaintiffs and their attorney are doing exactly the same things, as they develop their own strategy. For now, both sides are playing the litigation game outside of the courtroom—both sides are developing their "game plan."

Your attorney has a duty to help you formulate the strongest defense possible. To that end, your attorney can and will "coach" you in a variety of acceptable ways. For example, your attorney might:

Use interviewing techniques that stimulate your memory, such as asking you to relate events chronologically

Conduct interviews at the scene of material events

Ask you to write down, in your own words, your version of important events related to the case

In addition, your attorney will coach you by fully explaining the charges against you, and presenting as much as is known about the plaintiff's "theory of the case" and probable strategy. You need this kind of information so you can provide your attorney with a complete version of the events that doesn't leave out information that will be helpful to your defense.

Throughout the process of the development of your defense strategy, you may experience what we call the "sympathetic detachment" of your attorney. This means that he or she purposely distances himself or herself, psychologically, from you and your case. Effective attorneys recognize the difficulty they can experience if they become so closely associated with their clients that their objective judgments are impaired. Note, too, that while your attorney will be faithful to your lawful objectives, he or she has an overriding duty to the legal system and the public good, and can't foster expectations that are unrealistic or frivolous.

At the end of the process, you and your attorney should be armed with a carefully crafted defense strategy that will be made public in court, as the two opposing parties each present their own version of the truth.

> **Case Study Reference # 7**
>
> In Annie's case, the defendants' attorney, Stephen White, needed answers to many questions before he could formulate and finalize his defense strategy. For example:
>
> - What can we do, say, or provide to mitigate the importance of the lack of maintenance that allegedly led to the worn and broken bolt?
> - What can we do, say, or provide to mitigate the questions concerning improper supervision?
> - What can we do, say, or provide to convince the judge and/or jury that Annie's injuries were caused by an unforeseeable accident, not anyone's negligence?
> - What can we do, say, or provide to convince the judge and/or jury that neither school district employees nor school employees had any hand in Annie's injuries?

How can a judge or jury tell who's right? Both may be right or both may be wrong. The decisive factors are the facts and the interpretation of those facts, given the interpreters' biases, prejudices, and ideologies. The best interpretation is the one that takes all facts into account and agrees with them without any internal discrepancies or contradictions.

The Selection and Effectiveness of Witnesses

Witness Selection

Witnesses are a critical element in a lawsuit. Without witnesses, it would be your unsubstantiated word against the plaintiff's. Witnesses provide the judge and/or jury with the clearest possible understanding of the facts of the case, enabling them to make a just

Case Study Reference #8

In Annie's case, it was inevitable that, through the discovery process, the attorneys for both parties would zero in and focus on the same foundational issues and points of law, albeit from opposite perspectives:

- What constitutes an appropriate duty and standard of care regarding maintenance of equipment
- What constitutes an appropriate duty and standard of care regarding supervision of children at play on the playground
- Whether one could predict the potential long-term effects of the accident on Annie and her parents.

At trial, the attorneys for both parties planned to look at the facts of the case, as reported by witnesses, and the physical evidence to build their case—for the plaintiffs, negligence; for the defendants, appropriate and adequate care.

Case Study Reference #9

In Annie's case, the litigants found a number of expert witnesses who could verify (defendants) or dispute (plaintiffs) the appropriateness or inappropriateness of playground supervisory assignments and playground maintenance practices, and the extent of Annie's immediate and long term physical and psychological injuries.

decision. It's imperative that you and your attorney identify the set of witnesses who can best describe the situations listed in the Complaint and effectively make your case regarding the issues in question. The most important witnesses are those who have direct knowledge of the facts of the case, but witnesses who can address the secondary or underlying issues of the case (i.e., experts) can also have an important impact on the outcome of the trial. As a defendant in a lawsuit, you need to work closely with your attorney to identify potential witnesses who will be seen by the judge and/or jury as credible and unbiased, and who can present their testimony on your behalf in an effective manner.

There are four basic classifications of witnesses: expert, predicate, character, and fact. In Chapter Ten, we'll examine the role and function of the expert witness as a person who has made a voluntary decision to become involved with the court process by offering testimony, based not on direct knowledge of the issues in dispute, but on his or her expertise in a relevant field.

A second classification of witnesses is the predicate witness. A predicate witness has no personal knowledge of the facts of a case, but can establish the legal predicate (foundation) for the admissibility of evidence.

A third classification of witnesses is the character witness. A character witness may be called to testify to an admissible character trait of the defendant, another witness, or the plaintiff.

The fourth category of witnesses is the fact witness—someone who has direct knowledge of the events that led to the suit.

Generally, witnesses fall into one of three attitudinal categories, best described as friendly, neutral, or adverse. Your attorney's approach in questioning a witness will be noticeably different depending on the type of witness he or she is interviewing. In addition, we often find that some witnesses that we really want to testify on our behalf are reluctant to testify. Knowing how to obtain useful information from persons who are hostile or reluctant is a critical skill demonstrated by effective attorneys.

You need to be prepared to have potential witnesses refuse to testify. Among the common reasons that people who have information about a particular case may be reluctant to testify are that the potential witness:

> Believes you are guilty and doesn't want to provide information that might help you

> Doesn't want to get someone else (including himself or herself) in trouble

> Doesn't want to say anything that might hurt the complaining witness (e.g., the alleged victim)

> Doesn't want to admit that he or she wasn't paying attention

> Doesn't want to undergo the stress of having to publicly tell his or her story in a courtroom in front of a judge and jury, or just doesn't want to get involved

> May be embarrassed to reveal sensitive or personal information

> May not want to think about the act, event, or condition because it is emotionally painful

> May not want to lose time or money by getting involved in a court case

> May believe that his or her information is irrelevant

Case Study Reference #10

In Annie's case, Williams insisted that the school district's business manager be called as a witness on his behalf. She was able to provide documents, i.e., business office records, personnel records, time sheets, and the records of work orders initiated by Williams regarding work to be done on Red Ridge Elementary School's playground equipment, to support Williams' claims of proper maintenance.

Case Study Reference #11

In Annie's case, character witnesses were called by the defense to provide testimony to confirm the integrity, leadership, concern for the children, etc., for both the superintendent and Williams.

Preparing to Testify

Because of the frequency with which school leaders are subpoenaed, primarily as fact witnesses, the remainder of this chapter focuses

Case Study Reference #12

In Annie's case, Williams testified on his own behalf. Other fact witnesses that were subpoenaed or summoned for interrogatories and depositions by either the defendants or plaintiffs included the teachers and teacher's aide who were supervising the playground at the time the accident occurred. The school's custodian was subpoenaed and called to the stand by the defendants to testify to Williams' standing policy that all playground equipment be inspected on a routine basis and that he routinely completed this inspection. A teacher with long tenure at Williams' school was subpoenaed to testify to Williams' standard policies and practices regarding playground supervision, specifically, and to Williams' general attitude toward student safety and welfare. The plaintiffs subpoenaed teacher Jean Markley to confirm Williams' interrogatory statement that the supervision teachers were not following standard operating procedures regarding playground supervisory patterns at the time of Annie's accident.

on an examination of this distinct category of witnesses. As a potential fact witness, whether in trial or at deposition, here are some things you need to know.

Where other classifications of witnesses are generally allowed to offer opinions, fact witnesses are allowed to testify only about what they actually know as fact, for example, what they saw, what they heard, what they did, or what they told others to do, etc.

Generally, fact witnesses are called to testify by means of a subpoena. Five subsets of subpoenas include the:

Trial subpoena

Administrative subpoena

Subpoena for deposition

Subpoena to testify

Subpoena to present material evidence, i.e., records, correspondence, etc.

The subpoena identifies the time and place witnesses are to appear. Failure to comply with a subpoena is usually considered contempt of court. The receipt of a subpoena can be stressful, particularly if you haven't previously been a participant in a legal action, or have no previous knowledge of the process.

Attorneys for each side of the dispute identify witnesses who can provide testimony that is favorable to their case. The deposition process requires each witness to answer questions about his or her future testimony. Each side uses their witnesses to tell the factual story of their case. At trial, each side has the opportunity to examine its own witnesses and cross-examine testimony of the other side's witnesses.

Before testifying at a deposition or trial, you should think over what you know about the case. However, you shouldn't attempt to memorize your testimony, as it might seem "staged" or insincere to the opposing attorney, judge, or jury. The attorney who calls you as a witness will generally go over your testimony before the deposition and trial to be sure that he or she knows what you're going to say. However, your attorney is legally and ethically barred from telling you what to say. At the deposition and trial, the opposing attorney will likely ask if you've discussed your testimony with anyone, and may ask if you were "coached" by the attorney on what to say or not to say. If you were coached by your attorney, and this fact is uncovered at trial, it could severely weaken your credibility and could result in sanctions for your attorney.

At a deposition, the goal of the opposing attorney is to learn what each witness is going to say and what kind of witness he or she will be at the trial. The most important thing to remember is to tell the truth. You should never exaggerate or minimize your knowledge. Although you may be reluctant to say anything that will harm a friend or colleague, you are required to tell the truth.

Giving Testimony

When you're being questioned by an attorney, be aware that most effective attorneys use the T-funnel method of inquiry, in which they take you from general to specific questions on each relevant issue. Wait until you have heard the entire question before you answer. If you don't understand the question, ask for clarification. Generally, you should not answer questions with a simple "yes" or "no" unless you totally agree with the statement. If asked to expand on your answer, offer straightforward, declarative sentences. Don't "editorialize" or volunteer information that has not been specifically asked for.

If you don't know the answer to a question, don't guess. Simply state that you don't know. If you are asked a specific question that requires specific times, dates, or distances, you may give an approximate answer if you are not sure of the exact one. If after you answer you realize you made a mistake, you can ask permission to correct your statement. If a question is confusing or complex, you may break it down and answer one point at a time. Although the trial process may be new to you, the person asking you the questions is likely very

Case Study Reference #13

In Annie's case, even before the trial—during the discovery phase of the litigation—we saw a classic example of "volunteering" more information than the question asks, in Williams' "Interrogatory Excerpts," lines 235-238 (Chapter 3) where Williams provides (admits) information that could be detrimental to the defendants' case.

experienced at getting at the truth of a statement. Perjury is not an option for you.

Because our system of justice is adversarial, don't be surprised if your testimony is challenged under cross-examination. Some of these challenges may be rather forceful. It's important to remember not to take cross-examination personally. The lawyer for the other side may try to score points with the jury by baiting you into losing your temper. He or she may attempt to unnerve you by being rude, hostile, brusque, or abrasive. Your credibility may depend on your not losing your temper or becoming defensive or sarcastic.

A little preparation for testimony may prevent difficulty for you during a deposition or on the witness stand. First, however, let's examine the "personal qualities" you bring to the courtroom: your demeanor and deportment.

Demeanor is the manner in which you present yourself, the way in which you outwardly manifest your personality or attitude, and your style and essence of communication (especially verbal). Deportment includes your characteristic posture and your customary ways of moving and gesturing when addressing others. Both are primarily molded by your upbringing and training.

When testifying, whether in depositions or in the courtroom, you must have a positive demeanor, and demonstrate the kind of deportment that reflects your personality and position as a school leader, especially as it relates to the case at hand. What you have to say is important, but the way you say it, and the way you present yourself, have a lot to do with the believability of your testimony. You need to exhibit personal and professional conduct and bearing and an appearance that conforms to the conventions, proprieties, and mores of the education profession as well as the greater community.

Be courteous to all of the attorneys involved, regardless of whose side of the issue they're supporting, and respectful of the judge and members of the jury. Don't argue with any of the attorneys or the judge. Don't interrupt the attorneys or the judge and, of course, don't be contemptuous. Wisecracks or superficial remarks do nothing to bolster your position, and can undermine your testimony.

Use words and gestures, and act in ways, that are consistent with, and exemplify, a genuine (believable) respect for the rights and dignity of others. Act in a consistent and ethical manner. Finally, model the desirable leadership qualities of integrity, self-respect, self-confidence, vision, patience, perseverance, and courage. These are the qualities that people, including judges and juries, expect to observe in leaders.

Below is a list of general tips that may be helpful to you in preparing to testify. First however, the following three admonitions predominate: (1) Listen carefully to each question. (2) Don't read anything more into it than it asks, and answer only the question asked. (3) Remember that once you've said something, it becomes part of the record.

Take time to think about your answer. Don't allow yourself to be rushed into answering. Speak clearly. Be straight and precise with your answer. Remember that an effective cross-examiner often asks the same question in several different ways. Make sure your answers are consistent. Don't be afraid to say, "I don't know the answer to that question," or, "I don't remember." Don't make things up or guess.

Don't just accept the words of the attorney. If the words aren't exactly right, and make you uncomfortable, rephrase the question and your answer, using your own words. Be aware that the attorney who is cross-examining you may be trying to "spin" your testimony his or her way. Keep your testimony factual.

Don't object to answering a question, even if you think it is improper. If the question is improper, your attorney will object to it. If the judge interrupts you, or if one of the attorneys makes an objection, stop answering immediately. Wait until the judge directs you to answer.

Generally, you need to focus on the attorney asking the questions, but don't hesitate to look at the jury when answering an important question. Your attorney will advise you on any methods that he or she might want you to employ to assist you in "connecting" with the jury.

Finally, remember your demeanor and deportment at all times when you're in the court building. Don't talk about the case while you're in the building or on the grounds, except when you are on the witness stand or in a closed room with your attorney. Don't talk to any of the jurors or other witnesses if you see them in the building or in any other public place during the proceedings.

6

Courtroom Environment: You May Feel Small

In *As You Like It,* William Shakespeare said, "All the world's a stage, and all the men and women merely players." This couldn't be more true than when we're talking about the courtroom environment. We've all "experienced" the courtroom as it is presented in fictionalized form in motion pictures and television dramas and, in recent years, in actual trials televised live for our edification. Courtrooms are places in which critical issues are decided and lives can be forever changed. And whether our experience is based on fictionalized or real-life courtroom dramas, we've learned that life-altering legal decisions can turn on small missteps by a witness or procedural errors by an attorney.

Courtrooms are places in which the architecture, physical trappings, and procedural rules create barriers to keep participants apart and control the nature of their interactions. In this environment, the officers of the court (judge, plaintiff's and defendant's attorneys, bailiff, clerks, etc.) have the upper hand. Other participants (defendants, witnesses, even the jury) are frequently put at a disadvantage by the unfamiliar surroundings and may feel threatened by the fact that they are playing a game in which they don't know all the rules and, therefore, lack meaningful control of their destinies.

While we may enjoy watching a courtroom drama unfold as spectators, most of us never want to be players in such a drama. In this chapter, we take a closer look at various elements of the courtroom environment to demystify them and make the courtroom a more accessible and comfortable environment. Franz Kafka (1925/1968, p. 103) said, in *The Trial*, "By the end one gets quite used to it. By the time you've come back twice, you'll hardly notice how oppressive it is here." The following discussion is designed to save you the first two trips.

The Courtroom's Physical Design

Whether of traditional or modernistic design, the physical layout of the courtroom, including its furniture, lighting, acoustics, and entrances/exits, contributes to its ceremonial aura and effectively controls the actions and interactions that take place within its walls. Everyone who enters a courtroom is confronted by a place where subdued lighting, uncomfortable chairs, hollow acoustics, and, often, ornate hardwood or marble walls create an environment of solemnity and respect—not unlike the atmosphere associated with religious proceedings. The symbolic and theatrical features of the courtroom are designed to communicate a sense of seriousness and sobriety. And the United States flag and state and county insignia that are usually placed behind the judge implicitly communicate the patriotic nature of the authority of law. The contextual devices of the courtroom not only communicate authority, but also tend to mystify it "through the use of ultimates in order to rhetorically transcend the material world and to spiritualize a very secular sort of power" (Meisenhelder, 1981, p. 53).

The seating arrangements and spatial organization of the courtroom define hierarchical zones. The presiding judge is positioned at the highest point in the room, generally triangulated between the jury and the adversarial players (the plaintiff or prosecutor, the defendant and their attorneys). The judge's bench not only symbolizes the judge's authority, but puts him or her literally "above the fray" and out of reach, except when attorneys are formally invited to approach the bench. The adversarial teams are seated at separate tables, physically distanced from one another, and equidistant from the judge's bench, which they face. They and the other participants in the legal action are separated from non-participants by a railing—they are "before the bar." The jury is segregated in its own area of the courtroom, generally behind another railing or partition and off to one side of the room, where they can observe, but not participate in, the interactions between the adversaries. The witness box, usually beside the judge's bench, faces the courtroom and is frequently elevated a bit to ensure all participants can clearly see the witness as he or she testifies. Only "official" participants are authorized to enter the formal area of the courtroom. The general public is restricted to seating at the back of the courtroom.

Access to the formal area of the courtroom is controlled by a gate through which people may pass only when invited or compelled to enter. Other access to the formal courtroom exists through concealed doorways that are often indistinct from the surrounding walls. These hidden doorways lead to private areas that are used exclusively by courtroom personnel (judge, jury, clerks, court reporter, security officers, etc.). Movement into the courtroom from the "backstage" areas is privileged. It is through one of these concealed doors that the judge makes his or her ceremonial entrance into the courtroom. Jurors enter and exit the courtroom through another of these doors, so that they don't come in direct contact with other participants in the trial or the general public.

The layout and spatial design of the courtroom formalizes and constrains interaction among the participants in a trial. It also defines the status of the various participants. The elevation of the judge's bench and the judge's private entrance to the courtroom signify his or her status as the most important and prestigious person in the room. If you are the defendant, you are seated, with your attorney, below and facing the judge. You are inside the bar of the courtroom, but you may not move freely around the courtroom as the official agents can. Your position and, it should be noted, that of the plaintiff as well, denotes your subordinate position in the proceedings. As a person accustomed to exercising power, this may feel degrading and more than a little uncomfortable to you.

Rituals and Rhetoric

Among the foundational tenets of American jurisprudence is the right of defendants to a fair trial, briefly defined as the opportunity to face their accusers, hear the evidence against them, cross-examine witnesses, present evidence in their own defense, and have their case decided by an impartial judge or a jury of their peers. To ensure that trials are fair, there must be order in the courtroom, and both our federal and state court systems use rituals and rhetoric to create and maintain order. More specifically, courtroom rituals and rhetoric are designed to assign legitimate authority, define appropriate decorum, establish procedures to regulate the flow of information, and control the physical interactions of the participants. As is true in our legislative chambers and government executive offices, order and civility in the courtroom are seen as key to a fair exchange of information and legitimate, well-considered, just decisions.

Legitimacy exists when the definition of power provided by a body or described by an environment is accepted by the constituent audience. For the purposes of this book, we define authority as a subset of power, in which obedience to commands occurs because both the issuer and the commands are seen as legitimate. Lyman and Scott (1975) defined authority in the courtroom as a form of impression management. They further noted that the courtroom context and the official participants in it (judge, attorneys, clerks, etc.) can be considered sources of control—commanding compliance with rules of proper conduct and decorum.

The rituals of the courtroom begin with the formal entrance of the judge, signaled by a court officer, the bailiff, loudly announcing, "All rise!" The judge then enters the room while everyone present stands in silence in deference to his or her rank. All subsequent actions of participants in the trial are then taken only on the command of, or with the express permission of, the judge.

Judges traditionally wear black robes that emulate to those worn by both priests and medieval scholars, symbolizing spiritual high-mindedness and unassailable knowledge. The judges' robes communicate that they are to be treated with reverence and respect. The other officials of the court traditionally wear their "Sunday best" attire or the starched uniform of their office to signify their membership in the company of the legal elite. As a defendant, you are expected to dress for the occasion, not only to express your respect for the judge, the court, and the process, but also to confirm your status as a well-respected, upstanding, professional member of society.

The distinctive rhetoric of the courtroom merges with its rituals throughout the trial, as official participants refer to each other in a ceremonious and formal manner that ensures the civility of their interactions, while confirming each participant's relative status. For example, the judge is referred to as "your honor" and "the court"; attorneys as "learned counsel," "opposing counsel," or "learned colleague"; the bailiff as "court security officer"; police officers by their respective ranks; jury members as "ladies and gentlemen." In contrast, as the defendant, you will not be granted the same respected status. You may find yourself depersonalized and reduced to "the defendant" or "that man/woman."

Another rhetorical ritual of the courtroom is that the judge generally directs questions about the defendant to the defense counsel, ostensibly ignoring the accused. As the defendant, you might find extremely frustrating the fact that you can't directly address the court during hearings or a trial. However, the court's rationale for limiting your ability to speak on your own behalf is to prevent you from making any potentially incriminating remarks.

Yet another important rhetorical ritual of the courtroom is oath taking. When they are impaneled, jurors are required to raise their right hands and recite a pledge to hear the evidence and make their decision in an unbiased manner. Witnesses, when called to testify, take an oath that the testimony they give will be "the truth, the whole truth and nothing but the truth." Some courts require that the oath be taken "so help you God," invoking a powerful deity to witness testimony and assist in judgment (Bennett & Feldman, 1981). Oath taking acts as a rhetorical reminder of the majesty and the reverent nature of the courtroom.

The most active participants in a trial are the attorneys who represent the plaintiff(s) and the defendant(s). It is their job to present the evidence on which the case will be decided. Neither you, as the defendant, nor the jurors are allowed to question or cross-examine witnesses. Only the attorneys and the judge may officially confront the evidence. Following codified rules of evidence and courtroom procedures, attorneys introduce their respective sides of the case in their opening remarks and in their examination of the evidence and witnesses. The plaintiff's attorney will describe you as, and marshal evidence to prove that you are, morally reprehensible and accountable for the alleged misconduct, while your defense attorney will work to develop and prove a positive image of you and your actions or inactions, and identify any mitigating circumstances that should be considered.

Litigation attorneys are trained in methods—the rhetoric—of witness interrogation. They are skilled at framing their questions to witnesses, both to elicit persuasive, in-depth narratives and to carefully restrict responses. Official witnesses (police officers, experts, etc.) are also trained, or appropriately experienced, to testify effectively to promote their specific version of the truth. The development of evidence or discrediting of evidence presented can be a slow, painstaking process, but the rules of evidence are carefully designed to ensure that both sides of the lawsuit have equal opportunity to prove their cases to the judge and/or jury.

During the presentation of evidence, both the plaintiff's and the defendant's attorneys make use of another important rhetorical device, formal objections. Objections on either side are usually employed to argue an evidential issue, or to build a record of errors in the trial on which an appeal can be based. Regardless of the legal goal of the objection, these ceremonial protests, or interruptions, are rhetorical devices often used by attorneys to confuse the issue or disrupt testimony. Attorneys use objections to discount damaging testimony and evidence and to throw the opposition off balance. Through officially sanctioned objections, the attorneys may limit or cloud an issue, thereby exerting control over what the judge or jury hears and may consider in deciding the issue or case.

To understand the courtroom environment, it may be helpful to think of a trial as an elaborately staged and choreographed, but very serious and inherently antagonistic, "theatrical production," one that is carefully scripted and professionally acted to promote the clearest presentation of evidence on both sides so that a just verdict can be reached. Each of the principal "actors" in the production has a clearly defined role to play. The judge's role is to ensure that all of the action conforms to the "script"—the standards of courtroom procedure, the rules of evidence, and the letter of the law. The role of the attorneys, both for the plaintiff and the defendant, is to present the evidence that supports their party's version of reality in a clear and compelling manner and to discredit any evidence that doesn't. The jury's role, if there is a jury, is to weigh the evidence to determine the facts of the case and reach a verdict based on the relevant principles of law, as instructed by the judge.

As the defendant, your role is a subtle, but important one. With the exception of the brief time you may spend giving testimony, you will generally be an inactive participant in the trial. And yet, you will be under constant scrutiny by the lawyers, witnesses, judge, and jury. Your role, then, is to create, in the eyes of the court, the solid perception of yourself as professional, knowledgeable, respectable, upstanding, and innocent. Your comportment and dress can shape others' impressions of you. The "face" you show to the court informs others about your attention to, and attitude toward, the trial and the situation that brought it before the court.

Attorney Rhetoric and Jury Persuasion in the Courtroom

Edward Bennett Williams, a celebrated trial lawyer and influential Washington insider, whose clients ranged from teamsters' leader James R. Hoffa to Senator Joseph McCarthy, suggested that trials are like dramatic presentations in which the lawyer is producer, director, actor, and stage manager, but all, he noted, within the demanding constraints of the evidence and the law.

As educators and leaders, you know that much of your effectiveness lies with your ability to assume your role and communicate the importance of education and discipline to parents and students. You know that effective speaking, rhetoric, and a certain amount of drama are major components of your success.

The same is true of effective trial attorneys. They understand the importance of drama and rhetoric as art and science. While they may not have studied the writings of Aristotle—who, in the fourth century B.C., diagrammed the structure of persuasive discourse—or mastered the text of Quintilian's *Institutio Oratoria* to discover his belief that the study of rhetoric is the center of any enlightened system of education, they know that both rhetoric and drama are essential tools in the courtroom.

In the courtroom, attorneys practice the traditional and fundamental concepts of "Courtroom 101"—the principles of presentation and argument—that have been validated through centuries of practical experience. By adhering to this professional tradition, effective attorneys confirm their role in achieving justice. They demonstrate that it's easier to act themselves into right thought than to think themselves into right action. They understand that the triers of fact perceive whole stories and that the way the story is told makes all the difference. The most successful attorneys maintain the long line of the story they're telling through the milieu of witnesses, conflicting scenarios, and often-interrupted courtroom procedures.

So, if, during meetings, your attorney at times seems a bit distracted, he or she is probably "trying" your case as you talk. He or she is thinking about the trial as a whole, considering which materials (witnesses, evidence), tools (arguments, questions), and techniques (leading questions, styles of discourse) will be most successful, and designing the theatrical presentation that will most effectively promote your case.

Many attorneys believe that, in a jury trial, jurors reach a verdict with their right-brains, and then endorse these decisions with their left-brains. In other words, jurors use their emotions to decide the case and then explore the evidence to authenticate their emotional reactions on an intellectual basis. The key to courtroom success, then, is to persuade the jury, at an emotional level, of the merits of the case, using carefully crafted rhetoric and employing psychologically powerful persuasive techniques to shape the jury's understanding and assessment of the case. Litigation research demonstrates that jurors use an idiosyncratic approach to handling information presented in court. Repetition, key phrases, analogies, tone of voice, and other non-evidentiary factors have a powerful effect on jurors' subconscious thoughts and the way they process information and reach decisions. Among the rhetorical techniques attorneys use are:

- *Expectancy statements*, such as "You can expect us to show that. . . ." In psychology, this is called "gaining the selective attention" of the subjects. The goal is to encourage jurors to unconsciously look for information that supports the case argument and discount information that doesn't.

- *Rhetorical questions*, such as "What are the primary issues of this case?" or "Would we be here today if the plaintiff had demonstrated even a small amount of responsibility in her actions?" Litigation research indicates that introducing a counter-attitudinal message with questions leads to more focused processing of the message's content than introducing it with statements.

- *Colorful, even whimsical language* that is more memorable and has a much stronger impact on jurors than run-of-the-mill verbalization.

- *The Rule of Three* that an idea needs to be repeated at least three times for it to be remembered. For example, "Responsibility, responsibility, responsibility! If only the plaintiff had given thought to this basic concept of common sense this trial wouldn't be necessary." Studies in communication research show that people remember better, and agree more often with, a message that is repeated three times.

- *"Double bind rhetoric"* that characterizes the opposition in "either-or" terms that are equally negative to diminish juror sympathy for the opposition. For example, "Did the plaintiff injure herself because she was inattentive, or because she was careless?"

- *Analogies and metaphors* as appropriate to illustrate a point. Freud noted that analogies prove nothing, but make us feel right at home. For example, during the nationally televised final 2004 presidential debate between President George W. Bush and his opponent Senator John Kerry, Bush provided this illustrative statement regarding Kerry's proposed budget plans: "I want to remind people listening tonight that a plan is not a litany of complaints, and a plan is not to lay out programs you can't pay for." Kerry's pointed and equally illustrative response regarding the Bush administration's budget deficits, was, "Being lectured by the president on fiscal responsibility is a little bit like Tony Soprano talking to me about law and order in this country." Our favorite example, however, may be this one: "A smoke detector that stops working due to a simple short circuit is like a life preserver that keeps you afloat until it gets wet."

So, as you listen to and observe attorneys at work in the courtroom, remember Aristotle's fourth principle: a speaker must display an adequate level of emotion to sway an audience. Note also that the best attorneys are exemplary storytellers, providing a schematic road map for juries. Don't overreact to the rhetoric and dramatic presentation of either your attorney or the opposing attorney. Understand the game and the rules of the game, and play your part as directed by your attorney.

> **Case Study Reference #14**
>
> In Annie's case, the plaintiff's attorney painted the jury a vivid picture of a school district that:
>
> - Was not interested in the safety and welfare of its students.
> - Had fallen far below expected standards of duty and care and had professional employees who did not fit the "exemplar" status expected by the community, much less the profession.
> - Had professional employees who either recklessly or passively endangered the children they served by their disregard of all that is expected, right, and just.

The Adversarial System–Cross-Examination

The adversarial system of American jurisprudence is based on the assumption that true justice can only be achieved when two competent parties present their cases before an impartial trier of fact. It is up to the prosecutors and defense attorneys to properly present their cases. Experienced attorneys develop a high level of competency in the art of litigating. While the right to cross-examine each witness is fundamental to a fair trial and a useful method to discover truth, the process of discovering truth by cross-examination often looks like combat.

Because cross-examination is critical to the success of a case, lawyers learn the rules of the game through years of practice, while most witnesses only experience the process once. The rules of evidence in most states allow a witness to be cross-examined on any matter relevant to any issue in the case, including credibility. This is the area that is often most disturbing to those not familiar with the process. The scope of cross-examination is often expansive and not always limited to the scope of direct examination.

Once a judge has determined that a witness is competent, the jury must determine if the witness is credible. One function of cross-examination is to narrow, or expand, the testimony given on direct examination. This is generally non-confrontational and often rather friendly. The second function is more troublesome to the witness because its purpose is to attack the knowledge, recollection, or credibility of the witness. This is generally accomplished by exposing inaccuracies in the direct examination or by exposing the witness's bias or prejudice toward the other side of the controversy. The credibility of the witness may be challenged on the grounds of lack of personal knowledge, poor memory, bias, prejudice, partisanship, or corruption.

Attorneys establish the personal knowledge and memory of witnesses with questions about what the witness personally saw, heard, or experienced. They use questions regarding witnesses' mental states at the time of the event, their sobriety, their hearing, or their vision to attack their credibility. Some attorneys are very zealous in their cross-examination; others are more subtle. Regardless of the style, the purpose of the questioning is to confront the witness with information that shows he or she is incompetent, prejudiced, or corrupt.

Younger (1975) is frequently quoted as the leading authority on cross-examination. In his third of ten commandments, he states, "Ask only leading questions. Every question on cross-examination should put words in the adversary's mouth. All the adversary does is reply, in strict rhythm: 'Yes,' 'No,' or 'I don't know.' The leading question is the spoon to put the castor oil of unpleasant facts into the adversary's mouth." Younger also warns attorneys not to permit the witness to explain his or her statements. Commandment Seven states, "The effective cross-examiner controls the witness with leading questions. Permitting explanations is indicative of a loss of control."

Attorneys conducting a cross-examination often attempt to first gain the trust of the witness. They may start their examination in a very friendly manner, smiling and attempting to disarm the witness. In a case in which the testimony of the witness has been particularly helpful to the opposition, the attorney conducting the cross-examination may attempt to discredit the witness and minimize the harm the previous testimony may have caused.

References

Bennett, L., & Feldman, M. (1981). *Reconstructing reality in the courtroom.* New Brunswick, NJ: Rutgers University Press.

Kafka, F. (1968). *The trial* (W. Muir & E. Muir, Trans.). New York: Schocken Books. (Original work published 1925).

Lyman, S., & Scott, M. (1975). *The drama of social reality.* New York: Oxford University Press.

Meisenhelder, T. (1981). Law as symbolic action: Kenneth Burke's sociology of law. *Symbolic Interaction, 4,* 43-57.

Younger, I. (1975, August). *The art of cross examination.* Paper presented at the annual meeting of the American Bar Association, Montreal, Quebec, Canada.

7

The Trial

Once a case has proceeded through discovery and survived any pretrial motions, if there has been no settlement, it is set for trial. The most basic function of a trial is to settle disputes without violence. A case comes to trial because the parties involved disagree about the facts. The litigants in a trial have their "day in court" to publicly present their evidence and legal theories, and a judge ensures that only proper legal arguments and evidence are presented.

The primary role of a judge is to maintain order in the adversarial process and provide authoritative decisions on issues of law. The function of a jury is to resolve factual disputes. If a jury trial is either unavailable or waived, the judge assumes this function. At the end of the trial, the decision of the judge or jury (the verdict) is announced. The court then pronounces judgment, usually in accordance with the verdict. Sounds fairly simple, doesn't it? Actually, the procedures in a trial are pretty well-defined and, as a result, procedurally, a trial can be reasonably uncomplicated to follow and understand. In this section, we look at the component procedures to ensure your understanding of the processes.

Jury Versus Non-Jury

Prior to trial, the plaintiff and the defendant must decide whether the trial will be by judge or jury. A trial by jury can be waived (voluntary relinquishment of a known right) if the parties agree and the judge permits. (Note: Rules governing jury vs. non-jury rights vary from state to state.)

In a jury trial, the initial step is to select the jury. In federal courts, the judge selects the jury. In other courts, the jury is selected from the available pool of jurors through a process called *voir dire*. *Voir dire* permits each party to interview prospective jurors and challenge a juror's selection if they believe that the prospective juror can't or won't evaluate the evidence impartially. With all the prospective jurors assembled in the courtroom, the judge and the attorneys typically ask a series of questions and evaluate the responses. Attorneys for both parties are permitted to direct specific questions at individual prospective jurors, the responses to which might form the basis for a challenge.

Attorneys representing each party have an unlimited number of challenges "for cause" based on any responses to the questions that demonstrate clear bias or prejudice. A challenge prevents a prospective juror from serving. Additionally, each party has a limited number of peremptory challenges. A peremptory challenge permits a party to dismiss a prospective juror without "cause" merely because of unease about the prospective juror's ability to be impartial.

Presentation of the Case

After the jury has been selected, each attorney makes an opening statement—the formal presentation of the party's case. In a civil case, the plaintiff's attorney customarily makes the first opening statement. The defendant, through his or her attorney, then has the option of making an opening statement immediately following the plaintiff's statement, or of deferring it until the plaintiff has finished presenting evidence. The purpose of the opening statement is to outline the general nature of the case and to indicate the types of evidence to be offered. However, the opening statements are neither evidence nor proof. The trier of fact must consider only the evidence offered and admitted at trial in resolving factual issues. A matter attorneys often discuss in the opening statement is the burden of proof.

Burden of Proof

The burden of proof is the duty of a party to substantiate a factual allegation or position on an issue in order to avoid case dismissal, proceed to trial, and eventually prevail. In a civil trial, the plaintiff has the initial burden of proof. If the plaintiff fails to meet the burden of proof at the outset, the judge may dismiss the case, even if the defendant has not yet presented any evidence. Because of the initial burden of proof, the plaintiff introduces evidence to support the allegations stated in the Complaint. The plaintiff must convince the judge that there is sufficient evidence to meet this burden.

In civil cases, a party's burden of proof is met if an assertion is supported by a preponderance of the evidence (the party's assertion regarding an issue of fact is more probable than not), while in criminal cases, the prosecution's burden of proof is to establish guilt beyond a reasonable doubt—a much higher standard than simple preponderance.

Once the plaintiff meets the initial burden of proof, the defendant must attempt to disprove the evidence presented by the plaintiff. In other words, the defendant shares the burden of going forward with the evidence. Failure to do so could result in loss of the case.

Direct and Cross-Examination

The plaintiff proceeds by calling one or more witnesses. The witnesses swear, or affirm under penalty of perjury, that they will tell the truth. The witnesses then offer testimony under oath during direct examination by the plaintiff's attorney. After direct examination, each witness is subject to cross-examination by the defendant's attorney.

Direct examination is the initial questioning of a witness by the party who called the witness. Cross-examination is the questioning of a witness by a party other than the one who called the witness. The plaintiff's attorney may question the witness again on redirect examination to clarify points raised on cross-examination.

Evidence

Evidence, simply defined, means the facts, testimony, and physical substantiation or verification of the facts presented at trial to induce belief in or refute some claim. Evidence presented at trial must be reliable and relevant to the case to be legally admissible. During the trial, the judge rules on the admission or exclusion of both physical and testimonial evidence. If the judge disallows certain physical evidence or testimony, the attorney may preserve the right to appeal the decision on admissibility by making an offer of proof. An offer of proof is not considered evidence, but consists of oral or written statements by either attorney and included in the record.

The Record

The record comprises the pleadings and a transcript of the entire trial court proceeding. As a result of an objection and an offer of proof, the record will contain a reference to the evidence that the judge ruled inadmissible and that wasn't heard by the jury.

Objections and Motions to Strike

Objections can play an extremely important role in the trial. An objection indicates to the court that it may be making a mistake by either allowing or disallowing certain activity in the trial. If an attorney fails to make an objection, the client loses the right to raise that particular issue on appeal.

A motion to strike, simply stated, is a motion by either party to exclude a statement, testimony, or pleading from the court record of the proceedings. During testimony, an attorney may formally object to a question, answer, or comment based on a number of available grounds, and move to strike the offending words from the record. If the judge accepts the objection, he or she will order the language stricken and warn the jury to disregard the stricken language. Note, however, that juries have a hard time forgetting the information since "a bell once rung can't be unrung."

A motion to strike can also be defined as a motion presented to a judge by the opposing party after argument. The purpose of this motion is to request that the pleading's language be removed or deemed no longer effective, on the basis that the language (which could be an entire cause of action) is not proper, does not indicate a cause of action (a valid claim under the law), or is improperly formatted.

Motion for a Directed Verdict

The plaintiff rests after completing the presentation of its witnesses and physical evidence. When the plaintiff rests, the defendant may move for a directed verdict. A motion for a directed verdict (called a "judgment as a matter of law" in the federal courts) states that the plaintiff has failed to prove his or her case. To grant a motion for a directed verdict, the judge must be convinced that, after considering all the evidence, and with all reasonable inferences drawn most favorably to the party opposing the motion, the evidence is so clearly in the defendant's favor that "reasonable minds could not differ." If the judge agrees, a judgment of non-suit is entered in favor of the defendant. If the judge does not agree, he or she denies the motion, and the defendant must proceed to introduce evidence to contradict the plaintiff's evidence. The defendant calls witnesses and introduces testimonial and physical evidence in the same manner as the plaintiff.

When the trial is by jury, either or both parties may move for a directed verdict at the close of the defendant's evidence. Again, a motion for a directed verdict contends that the facts are so clear that reasonable people could not differ as to the outcome of the case. If the judge directs a verdict, the case is taken away from the jury. The judge then enters a judgment in favor of the party who made the motion. If neither party moves for a directed verdict, the judge may direct a verdict *sua sponte* (on his or her own initiative).

Final or Closing Arguments

After all the evidence is presented and before the case goes to the trier of fact for a decision, the attorneys for each party make final or closing arguments. In the closing argument, each attorney reviews the evidence produced by his or her side, and emphasizes its acceptability and credibility. Each attorney also points out the weaknesses in the other side's case. Note, however, that while closing arguments are not considered evidence, they can strongly influence the "picture" of the case that the jury takes into its deliberations.

After the closing arguments, the judge normally instructs the jurors as to the law applicable to the case. It is usually the jury's duty to:

- Determine the facts of the case
- Accept the law as instructed by the judge

Case Study Reference #16

In Annie's case, on the surface, the worn bolt alone was the key piece of evidence that could cause "reasonable minds to differ." Was it an "unforeseeable event" or was it an act of pure negligence? Was the playground supervision adequate or not? Even if the supervisors were standing five feet away from Annie, could they have foreseen the problem and protected Annie? A motion for a directed verdict was brought by the defendants, but the judge denied the motion, and forced the defendants to proceed with the presentation of their case.

Case Study Reference #17

In Annie's case, the plaintiffs might have asked for a directed verdict after the defense presented its case. However, some mitigating circumstances still remained—the same questions that were presented in Case Study Reference #16 were still unresolved by the facts of the case (for example, did Williams really do anything wrong?). The judge decided to proceed with the case and let the jury hash out the rights and wrongs. Remember, in this case, the jury had to decide the merits of all four counts as described in the Complaint.

- Apply that law to the facts of the case
- Reach a decision for the plaintiff or the defendant

In a civil lawsuit, the plaintiff must prove his or her case by a pre-ponderance (greater weight) of the evidence. In contrast, to convict a criminal defendant, the prosecutor must prove the facts beyond a rea-sonable doubt. The standard of proof is lower in a civil lawsuit and easier to achieve. The plaintiff's evidence must simply be more per-suasive than the defendant's evidence.

Verdict and Judgment

After receiving the judge's instructions, the jury retires to the jury room (or the judge to his or her chambers) to consider the evidence and reach a verdict. When the jury has reached its verdict (or the judge, his or her verdict), the Jury (or Judge) returns to the courtroom and announces the decision. A general verdict declares simply which party prevailed and does not include any special findings of fact. On the other hand, a special verdict consists of answers to spe-cific factual questions posed by the judge, without an attempt to reach a decision for either party. The judge then applies the law to the facts found.

Case Study Reference #18

In Annie's case, the attorney for the defense, from the start, had an uphill battle. Any time a young child is as badly injured during school as Annie was, and the plaintiff's attorney can show even the smallest amount of "blatant negligence" on the part of school officials, it's extremely difficult for the defense to counteract the evidence. The worn bolt was pretty strong evidence of improper maintenance.

The final phase in a trial is the render-ing of the judgment. The judgment is a judicial declaration of the rights of the par-ties (decision). Two kinds of relief may be provided by a judgment. First, the judg-ment may award the prevailing party costs, damages, and/or restora-tion of property (legal relief). Second, the judgment may order (or enjoin) the defendant to act or to refrain from acting (equitable relief).

Motion for a New Trial

After the judgment has been entered, either party may move for a new trial. A motion for a new trial states and argues that a serious legal error was made by the judge during the trial. If a motion for a new trial is granted, the case is again put on the trial calendar. If the motion is dismissed, the party that entered the motion may appeal.

Judgment Notwithstanding the Verdict

Often, after the judgment in a jury trial is entered, the losing party moves for a judgment notwithstanding the verdict (a "judgment as a matter of law" in the federal courts). In a motion for a judgment notwithstanding the verdict, the losing party argues that he or she is entitled to judgment under the law even though the jury rendered a contrary verdict. The judge will grant the motion and enter the judgment for the losing party only if there is no substantial evidence to support the decision by the jury. Substantial, as used here, refers not only to the weight of the evidence but also to its relevance.

Writ of Execution

The typical tool for enforcing legal relief is a writ of execution, a court order enforcing the judgment. The method for enforcing equitable relief is the court's contempt power. The penalty for contempt is typically payment of a fine or imprisonment for an indefinite period until the party in contempt agrees to perform his or her legal obligation.

Appeal

After entry of the judgment, either party may file an appeal. The loser is more likely to file, but sometimes the winner appeals, alleging that the damages awarded were inadequate. Appeal simply means that the party requests a higher court to review the case. The party who files an appeal is called the appellant. The other party is called the appellee or respondent. During the appellate process, the appellate court does not retry the case. No evidence is examined and there is no jury. The appellate court reviews a transcript of the case (the trial record) to determine whether any error of law or procedure was made. The appellate court reviews the complete trial record and may listen to oral arguments by the attorneys for both parties, who submit written briefs to support their arguments. Appeals are generally filed because the filing party believes that the trial court erred in one of the following ways:

- Improperly admitted or excluded testimony
- Ruled improperly on motions
- Misstated the law during jury instructions
- Misinterpreted state or federal statutes

After consideration of the record, the arguments, and the briefs presented, the appellate court renders its opinion/decision. The opinion may affirm (agree with), modify (alter), or reverse (set aside) the trial court's decision. The appellate court may also reverse and remand (send the case back to the trial court) for a new trial.

Efficiency and fairness demand that there be an end to litigation. Outside the context of the initial action and any appeals, a party may not relitigate either a claim or an issue that was actually litigated and determined. However, the initial litigation must have resulted in a valid and final judgment, on the merits of the case, by a court of competent jurisdiction. Such a claim or issue is said to be *res judicata* (a matter decided).

If the court in which the judgment was rendered properly exercised jurisdiction, courts in other systems are bound to respect the judgment. However, the judgment does not establish a binding precedent in those other systems. The Full Faith and Credit Clause in Article IV of the United States Constitution requires each state to give full faith and credit to the public acts, records, and judicial proceedings of other states. As a result, the Constitution permits a final judgment entered by a court in one state to be enforced in other jurisdictions without retrying the case.

8

Managing
and Surviving
Litigation Stress

As a direct result of the negligent acts of the defendant(s), plaintiff suffered permanent personal and psychological injuries, incurred and will continue to incur profound physical pain, emotional duress and suffering, and permanent disabilities, some of which may as yet be undiagnosed.

When words to this effect are contained in a formal Complaint alleging that, as a result of your actions or inaction, someone was injured or mistreated, it is often the beginning of a long, disruptive, and sometimes agonizing experience. The distressing events that led to the lawsuit were undoubtedly a source of anger, pain, and concern for you. And now, the lawsuit itself adds the burden of having to

Authors' Note: In our research for this subject we sought advice from the medical as well as the education community. A journal article titled, "Coping With Litigation Stress," by Thomas Hobbs, PhD, MD, and Gregory Gable, MA, (1998), published in the *Physician's News Digest*, provided some of the foundation for this section.

prove that you were not negligent in your actions or inaction. You may see the unfolding litigation process as an assault on your professional competence, reputation, and integrity. While you will never be in a position to choose whether to be sued, you can choose how to react and respond to a Complaint.

The Legal System: Perception Versus Reality

For most of us, the legal system is uncharted territory. Most of us have not dealt extensively with the legal process and, as a result, don't have in-depth knowledge or understanding of the way the system works. When facing a suit, understanding the game and its rules and strategies can help you avoid linking your professional confidence and self-esteem too closely to the litigation process and its outcome. Understanding two main points may be helpful:

- A lawsuit is just business as usual to attorneys and judges. To a judge who has 90 cases on the docket or an attorney who has been defending cases for 20 years, a case like yours is simply part of their jobs. You can minimize your frustration during the litigation process by understanding that attorneys, judges, etc., don't have, or at least won't share, their "feelings" about your case.

- The litigation process is a legal analysis very different from your day-to-day activities. Your education professional's mind works differently from the legal one. Your work emphasizes independent judgment and the best or most correct answer for multiple situations based on evidence that establishes the truth. In contrast, the legal mind focuses on what is in dispute, either legally or factually. Generally, there is no best or correct answer or established truth, only disputed facts and differing legal interpretations. The judge interprets the law, the judge or jury interprets the facts, and the judge or jury determines what is "true."

If you find yourself a defendant in a lawsuit, you need to learn to adjust your mindset to that of attorneys, judges, plaintiff's witnesses, and experts as quickly and as best you can.

Your Reactions to Being Sued

Two major factors that may leave you particularly vulnerable when faced with a lawsuit are your:

Lack of training in the litigation aspects of the education enterprise

Shock at being identified as a bad, ineffective, or error prone professional.

When confronted with a lawsuit, you may experience, as many others do, anger, depression, anxiety, insomnia, and increasing paranoia regarding those around you. Also common is a loss of pride and self-confidence. A normal response to such psychological reactions may be changes in the way you perform your everyday responsibilities. For example, you may begin to interact with your constituents in a more defensive manner, develop more rules and regulations, and eliminate or avoid high-risk activities. You may feel that you are viewed as less competent by others and get less satisfaction from your work. As an education professional, your identity has always been closely linked to your work. As a result, you're apt to see a lawsuit as a major assault on you and your integrity. The resulting lack of confidence can lead to "distancing" behaviors that may have long-term effects on your motivation, commitment, or professional image.

Many of the traits that make you an effective educator can make you a good litigant, especially when it comes to stress management. For example, in your ongoing efforts to keep your non-linear job environment as linear as possible, you have probably learned to suppress anxiety, detach yourself from emotionally charged situations, and consciously maintain your control over events. These coping mechanisms can often help you under the stress of litigation.

Stress Management Strategies

You will be better able to cope with litigation effectively if you can:

• *Accept what has happened.* Lawsuits can happen even when you have done everything possible to create and maintain a safe and effective school or district.

• *Distance yourself intellectually* and not view a lawsuit as a personal attack. Focus on the fact that litigation is simply a part of the education enterprise and not a commentary on your performance.

• *Maintain a full life.* Especially during the stress of litigation, make sure that your professional responsibilities don't interfere with your recreation and family activities.

- *Learn more about the litigation process.* You can channel some of your emotional energy and strong feelings about the lawsuit into helping your attorney prepare your defense.

- *Review the Complaint carefully* early in the process and discuss the issues honestly and openly with your attorney. Develop a realistic perspective of the various outcomes that could result from the lawsuit.

- *Share feelings with a confidant.* Although attorneys wisely advise defendants not to discuss the details of the case with anyone, it can be extremely helpful to discuss the disruptive emotional, interpersonal, professional, and social aspects of the litigation process and experience with a colleague or spouse who understands the unique environment in which you work.

- *Recognize that resolution of the lawsuit may be a slow, time-consuming process.* During the process, there may be peak times of activity, followed by months in which nothing happens.

The methods you choose to manage the stress of litigation will vary depending on your unique characteristics and your professional assignment. When challenged in a lawsuit, it's important for you to step back and reframe your perspective of yourself and your priorities in life. In doing so, you may be able to see the lawsuit in a new light. And, at the end of the lawsuit, let's hope you will be able to say to a colleague who finds himself or herself embroiled in litigation that although you had always considered a lawsuit something to fear and worry about, now that you've been through one, you know it's not such an awful thing. The experience made you realize that being a professional educator is what you do, not who you are. If the worst happened and you lost the case, you'd still be who you are and life would go on.

It's Never "Off the Record": Working With the Media

Because you are a "public servant" and a leader in your school, school district, or community, the media can be your best friend or your worst enemy. When an education-related incident occurs, or in a situation where you're involved in a lawsuit because of an incident, dealing with the media incorrectly can pollute or distort your message, creating an unwanted story that can easily develop into a public relations disaster—and can be used to discredit you in court.

If you become involved in a lawsuit, there are two very important things to remember. Don't speak or provide a written statement to the media until after you have:

Checked district policy or practice regarding media relations during a "crisis"

Sought advice from your attorney

There are some other important things to remember whenever you work with the media. Interactions between you and the media can be initiated in a number of ways. The most common are:

An organization-initiated press release

An invitation initiated by a superior

The intended or unintended actions of staff, students, or patrons

Public notices of legal proceedings

Whether the contact by the media is wanted or unwanted, you need to maintain and control the message at all times, regardless of whether the story is pleasant or unpleasant. Journalists can't be experts on every topic they cover. You should, with caution, assist the media in getting the facts of a story as accurate as possible. You are, after all, an educator, so assume that your primary task is to educate. The journalist is more than likely not an expert in your field of expertise. It is up to you to educate the journalist by providing the background to the story. Your secondary task is to tell a compelling story. When you prepare your press release or statement, make sure it's replete with facts concerning the incident. The more facts you provide, the greater the chance your story will be reported factually and fairly. Your ultimate job is to communicate your message to the intended audience—don't forget the purpose at hand. To ensure your audience's attention, you must hold their interest. Be prepared to display passion and confidence, and to show emotion. Be interesting to listen to and clear in your message. Effective communication is done person-to-person, so work to make a personal connection with the journalist.

Media Industry Drivers

All forms of media outlets have one goal. They are after a good story that will interest their readers, viewers, or listeners. To get and hold audience attention, the media always seek an "angle" or "hook" on which to hang the story. Don't assume news is limited to just the facts or truth.

Headlines are designed to grab the attention of the reader and will focus on the most newsworthy elements—drivers. These may involve racism, politics, violence, sex, religion, morals, and the law. Typical drivers for news media include stories that:

Are topical, timely, or fad-related

Have human interest (the story is person based)

Have novelty value or freakishness

Have high interest to the local community

Are about important or famous people

Lend themselves to the use of dramatic language and pictures

Describe a threat to security

Are sexual in nature

Are about survival

Have elements of conflict

Are emotive or suspenseful

Working With the Media

Be sure you are well-prepared before a media interview. You should assume that the journalists will have done some research about the incident or event, your school or district, and even you. Make sure you have a clear understanding of the specific details and relevant facts, and are well-prepared to answer the who, what, when, where, why, and how questions. Identify and focus on the key messages you want to communicate.

As you prepare to meet the media, remember that journalists can frame their questions in a variety of ways to get at the information they want. They often ask:

Short questions that demand a specific answer

Questions they believe the typical person in the street might ask

Questions that require a "yes" or "no" answer so they can follow up with the question "why" or "how"

The same question in an alternative way, if they feel you have not properly answered the original question

Questions framed in either a positive or negative way

During an interview, you'll help get your intended message out if you:

Listen to questions carefully and frame your answers thoughtfully.

Ask the journalist to repeat the question if you need more time (or need clarification).

Don't speak on a subject you know little or nothing about, and candidly admit your lack of information.

Never say anything "off the record." Treat everything as being "on the record" because the journalist likely will.

Never comment on or say anything confidential in a television or radio studio at any time. You don't know what is being recorded, even if you believe you're off the air.

When answering questions, remain as calm as possible and never lose your cool.

Always get to the point quickly and don't waffle.

Keep your mind clear of any thoughts other than your story and the message you intend to send.

Be careful of your reactions to obscure or threatening questions. A good journalist will hone in on your reaction. Just answer the question as straightforwardly as possible.

Keep your answers limited to three or four sentences or fifteen seconds.

To make your point, illustrate by example or with a list of rationale.

Only make statements and never answer a question with a question.

Try to relate to the interviewer, not just a camera or audience.

Never end with a moral or trite comment.

Journalists are people doing an important job—just as you are. Try to relate to them as fellow professionals.

PART III

Verdict and Analysis

9

Smith v. Red Ridge Unified School District No. 435 (Annie's Case)

Time Lapse

The time from date of the filing of the Complaint (see Chapter Three) to the date of the trial, Smith v. Red Ridge Unified School District No. 435 (Annie's Case), was approximately eight months. The trial, from gavel to gavel, lasted three days.

Jury Demographics

Twelve people from a pool of eighty-three were selected to serve in Annie's Case. Those selected and seated are briefly described below.

Eight women and four men were selected. Two alternates, one woman and one man, were named and attended the trial; however,

---

Autuor's Note: All names and events characterized in this chapter are again imaginary, as they were in Chapter Three, and do not reflect any real actions, incidents, persons, or places.

they were not needed. Of the eight women who were selected, four were mothers of young children (ages three to nine), three had grown children, and one was single. Of the four men who were selected, one was the father of a twelve-year-old child, two had grown children, and one was single.

Occupations of the female members of the jury ranged from full-time housewife and mother to full-time executive. Occupations of the male members of the jury ranged from unemployed to full-time executive.

Subpoenas Issued for Interrogatories and Depositions

Although not all of the people listed below were called to testify in court, they were subpoenaed during the discovery phase of the litigation. Each was asked individually to answer specific questions in writing (interrogatories) and each was summoned individually to provide testimony in deposition meetings.

For the Plaintiffs

Deposed under oath by plaintiff's attorney, Graham Sterling. Cross-examined by defendant's attorney, Stephen White. Recorded and filed.

- Individually, teacher/supervisors Markley, Matthews, and Tinsdale, who were on playground duty when Annie was injured.

Purposes of interrogatories and depositions: (1) To establish where each of them was, as opposed to where they should have been, when Annie was injured. (2) To establish playground supervisory assignments as "dispersed" as opposed to "gathered in one place." (3) Any other factual information that could assist the plaintiff's overall case (case-in-chief).

- Individually, Blaine Edwards, Director of Maintenance, Red Ridge Unified School District No. 435.

Purposes of interrogatory and deposition: (1) To establish "routine" districtwide maintenance versus school-site-originated work order maintenance patterns regarding the school district's playground equipment. (2) To establish district policy, if any, concerning playground maintenance. (3) Any other factual information that could assist the plaintiff's case-in-chief.

- Individually, Kathleen Henshaw, Assistant Superintendent of Business Management, Red Ridge Unified School District No. 435.

Purposes of interrogatory and deposition: (1) To establish "routine" districtwide business practices regarding facilities and grounds maintenance. (2) To establish the routine practices for processing maintenance orders. (3) To establish the availability of time sheets submitted by maintenance personnel for playground repair requests. (4) Any other factual information that could assist the plaintiff's case-in-chief.

- Individually, Christopher Williams, Principal of Red Ridge Elementary School.

Purposes of interrogatory and deposition: (1) To establish supervisory assignment patterns, policies, and procedures at Red Ridge Elementary School. (2) To establish routine operating procedures regarding district maintenance versus school-site work order requests for maintenance. (3) To establish his role and responsibilities as principal/supervisor at Red Ridge Elementary School. (4) Any other factual information that could assist the plaintiff's case-in-chief.

- Individually, physicians Riley, Murphy, Sheik, and Thorton.

Purposes of interrogatories and depositions: (1) To establish Annie's immediate injuries following the incident at Red Ridge Elementary School. (2) To establish probable cause and effect. (3) To establish the extent of Annie's injuries. (4) To establish the extent of short and long term effects of Annie's injuries. (5) To establish the extent of pain and suffering, including emotional distress, regarding both Annie and her parents, as a result of injuries suffered following the incident at Red Ridge Elementary School. (6) Any other factual information that could assist the plaintiff's case-in-chief.

- Individually, expert witnesses, Greely and Sangore.

Purposes of interrogatories and depositions: (1) To establish expected professional standards of duty and care. (2) To establish acceptable standards of proper maintenance. (3) To establish expected professional supervisory standards, i.e., supervision of teachers by principals, standards regarding ratio of children to adults, and placement of adult supervisors during student group activities. (4) To establish their credentials as experts in the field of education administration. (5) To establish the experts' opinions, based on the evidence available, on the following questions:

> Were playground expectations reasonable and prudent considering the age of students, specifically Annie?
>
> Was the incident foreseeable?
>
> Were the children on the playground at the time of Annie's injuries properly supervised? Were the adult playground supervisors at the time of Annie's injuries properly supervised?
>
> Did school officials follow school policy? Did the school district follow specifications as outlined by the United States Product Safety Commission for maintenance of playground equipment?
>
> Were appropriate authorities notified?
>
> After Annie's injuries, did school officials conduct a thorough investigation? Were well-documented records kept throughout the investigation?

(6) Questions regarding any other factual information or personal opinions that could assist the plaintiff's case-in-chief.

For the Defendants

Deposed under oath by defendants' attorney, Stephen White. Cross-examined by plaintiffs' attorney, Graham Sterling. Recorded and filed.

- Individually, Gloria Hunsinger, sixth-grade teacher at Red Ridge Elementary School for 21 years.

Purposes of interrogatory and deposition: (1) To establish Williams' patterns of supervisory assignments regarding student group activities.

(2) To establish Williams' sense of duty and standards of care to students and parents in comparison with Hunsinger's personal expectations and experiences with previous principals she's worked with. (3) To establish Williams' duty and standards of care in building and grounds maintenance in comparison with Hunsinger's personal expectations and experiences with previous principals she's worked with. (4) Any other factual information that could assist the defendant's case-in-chief.

- Individually, Wilson Reynolds, Head Custodian at Red Ridge Elementary School.

Purposes of interrogatory and deposition: (1) To establish Reynolds' routine daily assignment, by Williams, to inspect all playground equipment and play areas. (2) To establish work order routines. (3) To establish Williams' sense of duty and standards of care to students and parents in comparison with his personal expectations and experiences with previous principals he's worked with. (3) To establish Williams' duty and standards of care in building and grounds maintenance in comparison with Reynolds' personal expectations and experiences with previous principals he's worked with. (4) Any other factual information that could assist the defendant's case-in-chief.

- Individually, Andrew Calkins, Chairperson, Urban Council (ex officio member of the School Improvement Task Force)

Purposes of interrogatory and deposition: (1) To establish the Board of Education's and the superintendent's commitment to child safety and welfare in the Red Ridge Schools.

- Individually, expert witness, Whitaker

Purposes of interrogatory and deposition: (1) To establish expected professional standards of duty and care. (2) To establish acceptable standards of proper maintenance. (3) To establish expected professional supervisory standards, i.e., supervision of teachers by principals, standards regarding ratio of children to adults, and placement of adult supervisors during student group activities. (4) To establish his credentials as an expert in the field of education administration. (5) To establish his expert opinion, based on the evidence and records available, regarding the school district's follow-up investigation of Annie's accident. (6) Any other factual information or personal opinions that could assist the defendant's case-in-chief.

- Individually, expert witness, Stone

Purposes of interrogatory and deposition: (1) To establish normal trends in school accidents to children and children's normal coping mechanisms for dealing with a personal injury at school. (2) To establish her credentials as an expert in the field of education psychology. (3) Any other factual information or personal opinions that could assist the defendant's case-in-chief.

Litigation Strategies

Based on the information developed during the discovery phase, the attorneys for the plaintiffs and the defendants identified the key points they needed to prove if their respective clients were to succeed at trial. These key points are outlined below.

For the Plaintiffs

- Red Ridge School District No. 435 is responsible for the upkeep, through inspection, replacement of parts, and general routine maintenance, of all its holdings, e.g., buildings and grounds, playground equipment, furnishings, vehicles, etc.
- Eyeball inspection is inadequate for evaluation of the structures or support parts of playground equipment.
- The district has no standard rules or regulations regarding playground supervision, and playground supervision patterns at the school were inadequate for the number of children at play when Annie's accident occurred.
- Accidents happen, but Annie's fall could and should have been foreseen and prevented through common sense knowledge of patterns of equipment failure and appropriate and necessary levels of supervision.
- Regardless of the good things for which the school district is noted, 37 playground incidents occurred during the 2005-2006 school year that could be attributed to negligence on the part of the district and its agents.
- Expert witnesses will explain the extent of Annie's injuries, the pain and suffering of Annie and her parents, and the potential long-term effects of such. In addition, experts will demonstrate the ineffectiveness of the school district's patterns of maintenance and supervision.

For the Defendants

- The school district can't be held responsible for acts of nature, in this case the normal wear to the bolts on the swing set due to the climatic variables (moisture, temperatures, abrasive winds, etc.).
- All district playground equipment is visited annually and visually inspected as a part of the district's routine maintenance program. The playground equipment at the school in question is also visually inspected daily as a part of the school's routine maintenance program.
- Playground supervision patterns at the school routinely meet or exceed district standards.
- Accidents happen and not all potential accidents can be foreseen.
- Past and present districtwide surveys demonstrate that a large majority of parents (93%) are well-satisfied with the district's concern for, and care of, their children.
- Expert witnesses will refute claims of both improper maintenance and supervision and harm to Annie's and/or her parents' long-term emotional stability as a result of the incident.

Witnesses Summoned to Appear at Trial

For the Plaintiffs

Margaret Smith, Mother of Ann (Annie) Smith

Peter Riley, MD, Emergency Room Physician on duty at Wake Center Hospital when Annie was admitted

Franklin Murphy, Jr., MD, Smiths' Family Physician

Bashir Sheik, MD, Chief of Radiology at Wake Center Hospital

Thomas Thornton, MD, Specialist in Plastic and Reconstructive Surgery

Graham Greely, PhD, Professor at University College, Specialist in Negligent Torts

Phillip Sangore, EdD, Professor at Highland College, Specialist in School Leadership

Jean Markley, third-grade teacher at Red Ridge Elementary School

For the Defendants

Christopher Williams, Principal of Red Ridge Elementary School

Wilson Reynolds, Head Custodian at Red Ridge Elementary School

Gloria Hunsinger, sixth-grade teacher at Red Ridge Elementary School

Blaine Edwards, Director of Maintenance, Red Ridge Unified School District No. 435

Kathleen P. Henshaw, Assistant Superintendent of Business Management, Red Ridge Unified School District No. 435

Glen Whitaker, PhD, Professor Emeritus at Shadow Grove College, Specialist in School Facilities and Supervision of Personnel

Rebecca Stone, MD, PhD, Director of the Children's Clinic, a non-profit organization developed by Dr. Stone to aid children and parents in the aftermath of personal life-trauma

Andrew Calkins, Urban Council Chairperson

Jury Verdict in the Trial of Smith v. Red Ridge Unified School District No. 435 (Annie's Case)

Count I: Negligence – Guilty and Liable.

Count II: Improper Maintenance – Guilty and Liable.

Count III: Improper Supervision – Not Guilty and Not Liable.

Count IV: Breach of Obligation to Provide a Safe Place/Duty and Standard of Care – Not Guilty and Not Liable.

Damages Awarded by the Jury

From Defendant(s) to Plaintiffs in Red Ridge Unified School District No. 435 Board of Education, et al.

Amount Requested by Plaintiffs in original Complaint: On all Counts—Compensatory and Punitive—$1,260,000 plus Legal Fees and Other Costs of Litigation

Amount Awarded to Plaintiff at Trial: On Counts I and II—compensatory damages in the amount of $80,000, punitive damages in the amount of $100,000, plus legal fees and litigation costs, estimated to be $72,000. On counts III and IV–not applicable.

The Defendants' legal fees and costs of litigation were estimated to be $102,000. All awards and expenses related to the Defendants in Smith v. Red Ridge Unified School District No. 435 et al. were reimbursed by the school district's insurance carrier.

Polling of the Jury: A Fact Analysis

The jury deliberated for four and a half hours. There was no question in their minds regarding Counts I and II. The school district was clearly negligent in not regularly and appropriately inspecting playground equipment. Plaintiff's exhibit Number 1, the worn bolt, was the key piece of evidence, Annie's extensive injuries notwithstanding, according to the jury. There was, however, lengthy debate regarding counts III and IV. Jurors felt strongly that Williams was a good principal, and that he had done everything possible to prevent an accident such as Annie experienced at his school. His record of maintenance requests and the custodian's inspection routine were more than adequate. In addition, his policies and procedures regarding supervision of children on the playground were clearly communicated and appropriate. The following are some of the comments jurors shared with Defendant's attorney following the trial.

• Juror # 5. "We recognized that a teacher or group of teachers charged with supervising the play of children must exercise a high degree of care toward the children. However, the teachers and the principal are not the absolute ensurers of the safety of the children. We could find no requirement in the testimony that supervision of the playground activities of some 80 children requires that each individual child be under constant scrutiny."

• Juror #2. "No teacher can observe every student at every moment on a playground. To look at one is to look away from another. As a mother with small children, I know this only too well. Although the evidence showed that one or more of the teacher/supervisors were looking in another direction, it didn't seem to me to be negligence, as the Smith's attorney wanted us to believe. Besides, how could the principal, the teachers, and the custodian tell that the bolt was so worn? They would have had to remove the bolt from the swing set and that wasn't their job. I loved the custodian's comeback when the attorney for the Smiths asked him if he had the tools necessary to remove and inspect the bolts. He said something like, 'I had the tools at home and could bring them to school, but the bosses downtown say you can't be on a ladder without a second person to hold it, and my helper doesn't come in until four o'clock, and then we have only one hour for both of us to replace light bulbs. Besides, they only give me stepladders and they don't do well in the soft stuff they put under swings anymore.'"

- Juror #7. "You could have had a dozen or more adults standing in a circle around Annie and they still wouldn't have been able to see what the bolt was doing. The people at the school didn't do anything wrong. It was the people in the office downtown that screwed up. It sounded like they had an 'it couldn't happen here' attitude."

We close this chapter with the reminder that cases like Annie's are, unfortunately, commonplace in schools across the country. No amount of precaution on your part will ensure the safety of every child or adult you come in contact with each day. However, precaution and foreseeability must be operative words in your leadership vocabulary—risk management is critical.

Remember that the principles of law and the legal methodology discussed in this book are basically the same whether the case is founded, as this one was, on a tort issue, or on a constitutional rights question, or personnel issue, etc. As we noted in Chapter Three, "the breadth of civil law encompasses case law of considerable diversity."

PART IV

Your Role as an Expert Witness

10

Serving as an Expert Witness

Expert witnesses play an important role in the course of a lawsuit by offering relevant opinions that move the case closer to resolution. Successful school leaders develop a great deal of expertise about the orderly operation of schools. In some cases, they become experts in specific areas of school leadership, such as special education, school finance, school safety, student supervision, employment, or student discipline. Serving as an expert witness is one way to contribute to the education profession by assisting the court to understand how schools operate and which policies, procedures, and behaviors are acceptable, and which are unacceptable. As an expert witness, you are not expected to be an expert in law. In fact, your opinions about the law are irrelevant and won't be admitted. Your expertise is grounded in your experience as an educator.

The opposing sides of a lawsuit engage experts to analyze the facts of a case and opine about specific questions. Because the opinions of the experts are important to the outcome of the case, it is critical for anyone considering serving as an expert to know what he or she is getting into. While most attorneys understand the roles and responsibilities of expert witnesses, we educators are often clueless about the function of an expert or consulting witness. Although no attorney or client wants his or her case to be the place where the expert "learns the ropes," in fact, most expert witnesses learn about the process "on the job."

Although serving as an expert can be professionally rewarding, in that you can play a significant part in helping the court understand the standards of the education profession, it is time-consuming, stressful, tedious, and sometimes seems interminable.

Types of Experts

Experts are either consulting (non-testifying) or testifying. The primary distinction between the two is that communication between a consulting expert and the attorney is privileged. For example, an attorney may want an expert to evaluate the merits of a potential case and make recommendations about various strategies. The attorney wants the expert to speak candidly about the critical issues and the strengths and weaknesses of the potential case. As an expert, you may be asked to review a series of artifacts and depositions, and offer your opinion regarding whether the actions in question met the acceptable standards of the profession. For example, was the policy, procedure, or action appropriate and adequate to the situation? What would be the expected consequences of the actions? In this type of situation, the attorney would not want these discussions to be shared with opposing council, and would retain you as a consulting expert. Among the many services that a consulting expert can provide are:

Advice on litigation strategy and preparation for depositions

Initial review of depositions and evidence documentation

Review and analysis of the allegations in the complaint

Review of applicable literature, including government safety and regulatory databases

Assessment of the potential economic impact

Preparation of expert reports

Design/preparation of trial exhibits

On the other hand, if you are retained to testify, the opposing attorney has the right to take your deposition. At the deposition, you would be required to produce all communication between you and the attorney, as well as all notes, memos, and every document that you used in forming your opinion. Whether you are a consulting expert or a testifying one, all written materials you provided to the attorney must be disclosed.

Occasionally, opposing counsel will attempt to have an expert disqualified by the court. The test for admissibility of testimony by a qualified expert is whether the expert's specialized knowledge will assist the trier of fact to understand the evidence or determine a fact at issue. The goal is to provide the trier of fact a resource for ascertaining truth in relevant areas outside the knowledge of ordinary citizens. The testimony must be relevant and unbiased. Once you are qualified as an expert, you may testify to all matters within your experience or training, and you are generally given reasonably wide latitude in the opinions and conclusions you can state. This latitude is subject only to the general exercise of discretion by the court concerning whether you are truly qualified to offer such testimony.

Expert Evidence

Experts are allowed to testify at trial and give their opinions on issues in contention if their specialized knowledge will assist the trier of fact to understand the evidence or to determine a fact at issue. A witness may be qualified as an expert by knowledge, skill, experience, training or education and may testify in the form of an opinion. Whereas scientific evidence has to be generally accepted as valid by the relevant scientific community in order to be admitted in court, opinions about policies and practices must be based upon specialized knowledge. Examples of specialized knowledge would include an elementary

Case Study Reference # 19

In Annie's case, expert witnesses for the plaintiff included all of the doctors who had contact with Annie as a patient. In addition, the plaintiffs called two experts (Greely and Sangore) to establish expected duties and standards of care regarding proper maintenance and supervision.

In contrast, the defendants called an expert witness (Whitaker) to refute the plaintiff's experts' testimony regarding maintenance and supervision. They also called an expert witness (Stone) to mitigate the plaintiff's medical experts' conclusions regarding Annie's long-term physical and emotional prognosis.

The plaintiffs challenged the credibility of witness Stone on the basis of conflict of interest. On direct examination, Stone testified that she couldn't observe any evidence to suggest Annie might suffer long-term emotional problems as a result of the accident. On cross-examination, plaintiff's attorney reminded Stone that just five years earlier, she had published documents promoting her clinic's services that stated, "All children who have been involved in serious accidents suffer long-term emotional trauma and may need long-term professional counseling services." As a result of this challenge, the plaintiff's attorney effectively nullified Stone's direct testimony for the jury.

principal describing the proper manner for conducting a special education IEP staffing in an elementary school, a superintendent giving an opinion on the standard procedure for checking on a candidate's prior work history, and a professor testifying about the usual procedures for evaluating a teacher's classroom performance. It is important to understand that the expert is not permitted to testify on commonsense knowledge or nonspecialized knowledge. Courts don't need the testimony of an expert to explain information that everyone already understands.

Conflicts of Interest

There are no hard and fast rules about what is considered a conflict of interest. Generally, a conflict of interests occurs when a person has competing professional or personal interests that would make it difficult to fulfill his or her duties fairly. More generally, it is defined as any situation in which an individual is able to exploit his or her professional or official capacity in some way. There are two types of conflicts of interest: "real" and "perceived."

In the case of a "real" conflict, the expert is not able to fulfill his or her responsibilities because of a prior relationship. For example, if you were asked to serve as an expert in a case brought against your former school district, or in which the defendant is a colleague who was employed by your district, or in which the district is the one where your child goes to school, it would be generally understood that you would have difficulty offering an objective opinion about the case. In such a situation, it would be prudent for you to decline the opportunity to assist with the case.

An example of a case of a "perceived" conflict might be a case concerning a factual situation that is similar to a situation about which you have publicly expressed positive or negative opinions. For example, if the situation concerned a First Amendment issue involving censorship, and you have written an article or editorial in which you expressed strong opinions about freedom of expression, you might be accused of having a conflict of interest.

In the case of a "real" conflict of interest, you should not accept the responsibilities of serving as an expert witness. If you believe you can be objective in the face of a "perceived" conflict of interest, it would be up to the opposing counsel to successfully challenge your status.

Agreeing to Serve

If you are contacted by an attorney, you should ask him or her to tell you about the case before you decide whether you are interested in serving as an expert. Obviously, you must remember that you are going to hear the case in the light most favorable to the client of the attorney who is contacting you. At this early stage, you won't know if the attorney is honest. Nor will you know if he or she is experienced in trying this specific type of case. You should try to learn the answers to these questions before you proceed. If you decide that you have the expertise necessary to contribute to the court's understanding of the issue, and that the attorney seems to be a person you'll be able to work with, you should then request all materials relating to the case.

The Importance of a Contract

Serving as a consulting or testifying witness is time-consuming, stressful, and demands that work be done on time. Court schedules change, new material surfaces, and attorneys change. When you agree to serve, you are making a commitment to the attorney and his or her client that you will complete the job. If you choose to serve as an expert, your first step should be to develop a contract that clarifies, exactly, the service you expect to provide and the amount you expect to be paid. Although a written contract will not necessarily protect you from an unethical attorney, it is important that you make clear your conditions of service and that your name may not be used without your written permission.

Consulting Fees

Fees that experts charge vary from region to region and from academic discipline to academic discipline. Some experts may charge more than you do, some may charge less. You should base your fee on your honest perception of what your time and effort are worth. You may want to contact several attorneys in your area and ask if there is a standard fee. Whatever fee you set, you should be comfortable with the knowledge that if an attorney believes that your fee is too high, he or she has the option of not hiring you to serve as an expert.

Most educators are inexperienced in billing for their services. Consequently, they are often reluctant to talk about money. However, you need to set a specific value on your time—an hourly rate. In addition, you need a clear understanding about who pays your expenses for overnight mail, phone calls, duplication charges, travel time, research assistance, etc. Be sure that it is clear that your fee is not negotiable and that you are not working on a contingency basis. Your testimony will be of little value if it appears that you will only get paid if the client that pays you wins the case.

Once you've set your fee, you should also require that a retainer be paid prior to beginning any work. It is not a pleasant or easy task to attempt to collect fees from a client who is unsatisfied with the court's decision, is unsatisfied with the amount of the settlement, or has recently suffered a financial setback.

Your Responsibilities as an Expert Witness

Report and Deposition

When you serve as an expert in a federal or state court, you may be required to provide opposing counsel with a report that contains a complete statement of all opinions you expect to express and the basis for these opinions. You may also have to provide the information that you relied upon in forming your opinions, your qualifications, a listing of all of your publications, the compensation to be paid, and a listing of any other cases in which you have testified as an expert, at trial or by deposition, within the past few years.

As the expert, you must sign the report, but there is no prohibition against you and the attorney working together to be sure that the report addresses the relevant issues. However, be very careful about attorneys who want to take part in the preparation of your reports. Be sure not to allow an attorney to lead you to a particular theory or conclusion. Such activity can seriously damage your reputation, credibility, and integrity.

A deposition is a process of questions and answers, given under oath, that are recorded verbatim by a court reporter. The deposition is generally taken at your workplace or a place convenient to you. It may be videotaped or audiotaped. The attorney that retained you will usually be present.

Prior to giving a deposition, you may confer with the hiring attorney to go over the substance of the testimony. However, it is inappropriate for the attorney to attempt to coach you on what to say. Some attorneys believe this preparation is important, others do not.

You need to remember that any communication between you and the attorney is discoverable. This means that any draft reports, memos, e-mails, or handwritten notes may be required to be produced.

Opposing counsel has the right to know what you are going to say at the trial and what influenced your opinions. Unless the attorney who retained you orders you not to answer a question, you must answer each question asked.

A word of warning: If you have written it, said it, or thought it, assume that opposing counsel knows about it. One of the ways a person becomes identified as an expert is by having numerous articles published in peer-reviewed journals. Another is by being invited to present papers at regional and national conferences. Yet another is by writing books and giving interviews. It is not uncommon for the attorney taking your deposition to ask if you agree with a specific statement, and then reach into his or her briefcase, pull out an article you wrote, or a speech you gave, 10 years ago, and quote your words back to you.

Although some depositions may be relatively short and focus exclusively on your report and your anticipated testimony, it is not uncommon for a deposition to last a day or more. If your opinions have changed over time, be prepared to admit this and explain why. You may also want to think about any coauthored works that may have been published. Did you and your colleague have specific responsibility for sections of the work? If you and your coauthor compromised on any issues for the sake of harmony, you may find yourself trying to explain why something in "your" article does not really reflect your thinking. Listen to each question very carefully, and expect to be quoted out of context. You have the right to clarify your answers.

Depositions can be thought of in terms of their metaphorical content. Depending on the personality and style of the opposing counsel, depositions can be described as a circus, a Broadway show, a well-choreographed ballet, or a little shop of horrors. Some depositions proceed in an orderly manner, with each attorney exhibiting grace and charm. Others are unpredictable, tension-filled nightmares that resemble a war zone. The majority of attorneys who take your deposition or testimony will be incredibly well-prepared and have a clear plan of action. Others may appear to have never heard of you, your report, or the case at hand. Of course, these attorneys may also be following their plans. Some attorneys sit silently through the entire deposition. Others seem to object to almost every question.

Although most attorneys use the deposition to discover what you are going to say and how you are going to support your opinions, others seem to view the deposition as the first round of a heavyweight fight. These attorneys seem primarily interested in learning how you will behave on the witness stand. Attorneys have been known to slam their fists on the table, shout, and use intimidation. Other attorneys come across as sarcastic and mean-spirited. Don't take it personally if an opposing attorney refers to you as a "so-called expert," or "hired gun." It is prudent to ask the attorney who retained you to tell you about the opposing attorney's style so you know what to expect.

After you have given your deposition, you should be given an opportunity to read and sign the deposition. Be careful that the attorneys do not waive this right on your behalf. You definitely want to have the opportunity to review the document for accuracy and to correct any errors.

The Trial

Most juries place a significant amount of weight on the perceived credibility of the witness. At the trial, you will be questioned about the substance of your report. The attorney who hired you will give you the opportunity to state your opinions about the case. The opposing counsel will attempt to discredit your expertise and the validity of your opinions. It is a fundamental principal of testimony that you may not testify regarding any conclusions that were not included in your report.

Points to Remember

You involved yourself as an expert to help the court understand what the standards are and your opinion regarding the various individuals' relationship to those standards. Because what you say may have a significant impact on people's reputations, livelihoods, community standings, and careers, it's essential that you not allow yourself to wander outside of your expertise. Don't allow yourself to be seduced into getting involved in a case that may be interesting but is outside of your knowledge base.

It is also important to make it clear, to all involved, that the opinions you express are yours and do not reflect the views of your employer. Although most education organizations provide released time for professional activity, you should inform your employer of your intention to serve as an expert witness, and give your employer the opportunity to determine if the activity is congruent with the mission of the organization and not in conflict with your primary duties. Be sure that you know, and conform to, any relevant employment policies. You never know when or where your comments will appear.

Although some experts have web pages, newsletters, or are listed with an expert referral service, most attorneys locate expert witnesses by reading court decisions, talking to colleagues, and reviewing experts' reports. Attorneys tend to select experts that have served in cases where the facts were similar to their current case and where the expert's opinions seem congruent with their analysis of the case. Consequently, it's not unusual for an expert to be asked to serve in plaintiff cases or defense cases. If you repeatedly serve on one side or the other, opposing counsel will likely attempt to portray you as an advocate rather than an impartial expert. This should not trouble you if you can document the basis for your opinions. It's up to a judge or jury to evaluate you and your opinions.

Finally, in the process of your testimony, specifically when you're being examined in court by the opposing party's attorney, you may be subjected to questions about your personal life. Remember, whatever role you're in—defendant, plaintiff, general or expert witness—you and your professional image are fair game for "discreditation." Be prepared, be tactful, and think before you speak.

PART V

Managing Your Risk of Litigation

11

Concluding Thoughts

The trial of Socrates is, without doubt, one of the most famous teacher trials in history. In 399 B.C., the 80-year-old philosopher-educator was charged with "corruption of the young" and brought before a jury of 501 of his fellow citizens, who found him guilty of subverting the established political system by encouraging his students to question authority. The story of the trial, as reported by Socrates' student Plato, is an example to all of us who have chosen education as our profession.

Another trial that lives on in history and seems to regenerate itself every time there's a debate about creationism theory ("Intelligent Design" in today's parlance), is the Dayton, Tennessee "Scopes Monkey Trial." The Scopes trial pitted perpetual presidential contender and fundamentalist orator William Jennings Bryan against the colorful and somewhat radical lawyer Clarence Darrow in a trial that H.L. Mencken reported to the world at large. Although Scopes was found guilty of disobeying a state law prohibiting the teaching of evolution, the effect of the trial was to promote the more scientific curriculum across the country.

Few education-related trials or legal questions emanating from our profession are as monumental as the trial of Socrates or the legalities and politics surrounding the teaching of evolution as opposed to creationism. The majority of challenges we face in court today involve everyday issues of the care and conduct of educators in fulfilling their duties of supervision and direction of students and employees in our school districts—all a part of the landscape in which law and education can easily intersect in our professional careers. Legal activism has found a home in the education enterprise. Not only are there more lawsuits against educators, there are also more diverse types of lawsuits aimed in our direction. Obviously, the best protection against litigation is preventive action. We educators are vulnerable because, like doctors, we deal with one of our most precious assets, human well-being. And, as is true with the medical profession, we are never far removed from the shadow of the courthouse.

While this book has focused, up to this point, on what to do if you're involved in litigation, other books we have written focus on what to do to avoid litigation. We prefer the latter. The business of a lawyer is not to win cases in court, but to keep clients out of court; we believe that the same is applicable to your role as a leader of education professionals. Almost every major case against educators stems from negligent conduct, uncontrolled emotion, or a simple lack of common sense—not from a lack of knowledge of proper conduct. And we know that "lack of knowledge" is never a winning defense anyway. We want you to be fully prepared to face legal challenges and that's what this book is about. However, we also would like you to avoid such challenges whenever possible.

We opened this book with a short review of the legal environment and an overview of the organization of courts to establish a foundation for the ensuing chapters. We close this book with another review we feel is just as important, a brief overview of some of the things that will help you avoid litigation by practicing preventive law to help manage your risk of litigation.

Accidents, incidents, or transgressions are organizational and management problems—not always, as you might tend to think, people problems. Regardless of the root causes of problems that may lead to litigation, such events are too often dealt with *ex post facto*, rather than through a well-planned, active program of risk anticipation and litigation prevention. You can help reduce your risk factors with a well-defined, proactive program of preventive law. A preventive law program is designed to regulate and manage human conduct to ensure a harmonious environment and strike a balance that allows individuals as much freedom as possible, while at the same time allowing the community to function without unreasonable interference from the conduct of individuals.

During the preceding century, changes in American culture have created numerous conflicts in society. These conflicts led to new and ever more challenging issues. Such issues required new laws. Needless to say, for you, as an effective school leader, to practice preventive law and risk management, it is imperative that you seek out and maintain a working knowledge of current laws that affect education. Effective school leaders don't wait for legal counsel to provide information. They take the time to read, listen to, and actively apply what they know to avoid harm to students and others and to short-circuit incidents that might lead to litigation. You should recognize liability as a consideration in your daily operations.

There is a tendency in many school districts to temporize and down play the significance of legal problems, seeking answers to such problems at the operational level rather than at the organizational level. School districts often rely on legal counsel only after they have gotten into trouble. That said, despite district initiatives or lack thereof, you can significantly reduce your exposure to liability by incorporating and practicing preventive law as outlined below.

The concepts of preventive law are illustrated by six general beliefs and tenets:

1. *An understanding of the substance of law limits an education organization's culpability and exposure.* In your day-to-day decision making, you need to understand the substance of law, which consists of both an understanding of the basic tenets of law and knowledge of current education litigation decisions.

2. *The proper application of procedures, informed decision making, and foreseeability reduces liability and environmental and organizational loss.* To be effective as a school leader, you must adhere to procedures and precedents established by law, exercise reasonable and prudent judgment in situations not directly addressed by the law, and integrate foreseeability (the art or science of intuitively knowing what might happen) when practicing preventive law, thus minimizing your exposure to liability and loss.

3. *Working with counsel reduces budget loss.* When you have questions about legal issues that are not directly addressed in established laws and procedures, you should consult legal counsel. Proactive school districts should allow their school leaders to do so, at district expense, within reason.

4. *Flexibility endangers system stability, but enhances conflict resolution.* Although you must strictly adhere to, enforce, and monitor all policies and procedures, you should also demonstrate flexibility and reduce

conflict (and avoid litigation) by fostering a school climate in which divergent ideas may be presented, respected, permitted to flourish, and channeled into productive results for the school or district.

5. *Knowledge of precedent, constitutional compliance, and public information needs enhances crisis and motivational management and monitoring.* You need to understand the legal ramifications of precedent-setting cases, and consider the significant protections provided to students, teachers, and others under various interpretations of enacted laws and the Constitution when making decisions. You should also recognize that it is often up to you to educate parents and others about how court actions influence the daily operations of your school or district.

6. *Leadership in the education enterprise must be coupled with leadership in preventive law.* Effective education leadership sometimes involves taking calculated risks when complicated situations warrant decisive action; however, any risks you take must be legal and must demonstrate a commonsense commitment to preventive law.[1]

Given the many decisions you make on a daily basis, the quality of your judgment can spell the difference between a safe and supportive learning environment and an environment that's ripe for legal intervention. In reality, your decisions are what education leadership is all about.

Note

1. The six tenets listed above, although edited for the purposes of this book, were originally published in greater detail in *The Principal's Quick-Reference Guide to School Law*, by Dennis Dunklee and Robert Shoop, 2002, Thousand Oaks, CA: Corwin Press.

Index

Accidents, 10–11, 71, 112
Administrative law, 20–23
  acceptable behavior and, 14
  common law and, 23
Administrators. *See also* School leaders
  leadership and, 16
  See also Leadership
  safety and, 11–12
  standards of care and, 8
  See also Standards of care
Adversarial system, 80, 87–88
Alexander, K., 10
Alexander, M., 10
Alternative dispute
  resolution (ADR), 29
American Association of School
  Administrators, 15
Answer, 54–55
Appeals, 59–60, 93, 97–98
  objections and, 83–84
Appellate courts, 27–28
Appellate jurisdiction, 25
Appellee, 60
Arbitration, 69
Arbitration, non binding, 30–31
Aristotle, 85, 87
Arraignments, 65
Assistant principals, 11–12
Attendance, 12
Attorney general, 24–25
Attorneys:
  closing arguments and, 95
  control and, 82, 84, 88
    See also Control
  courtrooms and, 79, 81, 85, 92, 94
  cross-examinations and, 76, 88, 93
    See also Cross-examinations
  defense strategy and, 69–71
  depositions and, 122–123, 126–128

  drama and, 79, 85
  fees and, 59
  interrogation and, 83
  jurors and, 92
  mediations and, 30
  objections and, 83–84
  pre-suit preparation and, 67–69
  respecting, 76
  rhetorical techniques and, 86–87
  successful, 85
  witnesses and, 73, 74, 75, 88, 121

Behavior:
  acceptable, 14–17
  leadership and, 16
  standards of, 20
Bench trials, 65
Bennett, L., 83, 84
Bethel School District No.
  403 v. Fraser, 17
Bill of rights, 20–21
Binding arbitration, 30–31
Bryan, W. J., 133
Burden of proof, 92–93
Bush, G. W., 86

Calkins, A., 113, 116
Case-in-chief, 59
Case law, 14
Cause of action, 53, 59–60
Child abuse, 13–14
Civil Action for Deprivation
  of Rights Act, 12–13
Civil laws, 20
Civil litigation, 51–52
Civil suits, 63
Class action, 62–63
Common law, 20–23
  acceptable behavior and, 14

CORWIN PRESS

The Corwin Press logo—a raven striding across an open book—represents the union of courage and learning. Corwin Press is committed to improving education for all learners by publishing books and other professional development resources for those serving the field of PreK–12 education. By providing practical, hands-on materials, Corwin Press continues to carry out the promise of its motto: **"Helping Educators Do Their Work Better."**